PRAISE FOR RACHEL HOLLIS AND
GIRL, STOP APOLOGIZING

"Rachel Hollis is a live-out-loud leader with a heart for helping women tenaciously chase their purpose and dreams without apology. Rachel's ability to share stories and principles with raw honesty inspires her readers to discover and take the practical steps that will put them on a lifelong path of personal growth."

—Dr. John C. Maxwell, author and leadership expert

"Ever felt stuck? Ever struggled to make time for your dreams—or struggled even to admit those dreams to yourself? In *Girl, Stop Apologizing*, Rachel Hollis points out the pitfalls, challenges, and excuses that stop us from achieving our aims. She speaks with refreshing (and often hilarious) candor about her own experiences and mistakes, and offers concrete advice about how to create the lives we want."

—Gretchen Rubin, *New York Times* bestselling
author of *The Happiness Project*

"*Girl, Stop Apologizing* is the life-changing guide (and permission!) we've all needed to dump our excuses, embrace our dreams, set boundaries, and gain real confidence and momentum in life. It's how to overcome a 'lifetime of people pleasing' and start crafting the vibrant, authentic life you deserve. This is a must-read for taking your destiny into your own hands. I loved every page!"

—Brendon Burchard, #1 New York Times bestselling
author of *The Millionaire Messenger*, *The Motivation
Manifesto*, and *High Performance Habits*

"Reading *Girl, Stop Apologizing* is like sitting down with a best friend who can speak deeply into the dark places you've been trying to hide and shines a light on them. Rachel has the ability to help you silence your inner mean girl while encouraging you to believe that you truly can change and become the woman you've always envisioned yourself to be. Rachel's gift is in giving you permission to not feel alone or ashamed of where you've been, while also giving you hope and a plan for what's ahead of you. Her voice in my ear has been a guiding light to pursue greatness and more for this one life I am living."

—Jenna Kutcher, photographer, podcaster, educator,
and host of *The Goal Digger Podcast*

"Rachel is the modern-day Oprah and female Tony Robbins! She provides a safe place for women to dream big and believe in themselves, while also giving the tough love all great moms give to their kids to take ownership of their life and providing the keys to succeed. Rachel is raw, real, and full of life. She combines emotion, humor, and straight-talk to make all of us believe and see how we can have the life we want if we've invested the time and learned how to get there. Get this book and *stop apologizing!*"

—Lewis Howes, *New York Times* bestselling author and host of *The School of Greatness* podcast

"Though energy-evoking, motivation alone isn't enough to actually move the needle in your life. Rachel Hollis gets this at the deepest level possible. *Girl, Stop Apologizing* is a true masterpiece that combines heartfelt inspiration with the perfect mix of tools and a framework that can allow you to effectively adopt new behaviors and skills in your life that create real and lasting change."

—Dean Graziosi, *New York Times* bestselling author, entrepreneur, and investor

"Rachel Hollis is a force of inspiration who is impacting the world on a massive level. Her unapologetic message of self-worth will continue to transform lives for many decades to come."

—Trent Shelton, author, motivational speaker, and founder and CEO of RehabTime

"Rachel is the leader in modern-day personal development for a reason. Her authenticity, vulnerability, and experience separate her from everyone else. She just knows how to 'get real' in a way that is unapologetically Rachel."

—Ed Mylett, entrepreneur, personal development coach, speaker and host of the *Ed Mylett Show* podcast

"*Girl, Stop Apologizing* is an unflinchingly relatable manifesto that is as unapologetic as it gets. Each chapter is an espresso shot that kickstarts your 'can-do-itude' and challenges you to reach further and higher to achieve your goals."

—Arlan Hamilton, founder and managing director of Backstage Capital

"It's time to truly embrace your greatness, and there is no better rally cry than *Girl, Stop Apologizing*. Unapologetic herself, Rachel is the fearless girl-friend you need to help you leap into the bold unknown and fulfill that big audacious goal you have been waiting to achieve. And that's a movement I'm thrilled to be a part of."

—Amy Porterfield, online marketing expert

GIRL, STOP APOLOGIZING

A SHAME-FREE PLAN FOR EMBRACING AND ACHIEVING YOUR GOALS

RACHEL HOLLIS

HarperCollins
LEADERSHIP

An Imprint of HarperCollins

Published by HarperCollins Leadership, an imprint of HarperCollins Focus, LLC.

Illustrations created by Annie Ludes.

ISBN 978-1-4002-0961-3 (eBook)
ISBN 978-1-4002-0960-6 (HC)
ISBN 978-1-4002-1506-5 (IE)

Library of Congress Cataloging-in-Publication Data

Library of Congress Control Number: 2018957777

Printed in the United States of America

19 20 21 22 23   PC/WOR   10 9 8 7 6 5 4 3 2 1

For my daughter, Noah.

May you live your life—without apology—in celebration of who God created you to be.

CONTENTS

PART III: SKILLS TO ACQUIRE

INTRODUCTION

WHAT IF . . .

When I originally started writing this book I fully planned on calling it *Sorry, Not Sorry*. And, yes, I was basing that title on a Demi Lovato song. In fact, I'd go so far as to say that the song was the impetus for this entire book.

Imagine, if you will, the late summer of 2017 when I first heard this jam. It was a sunny Monday morning. I know it was Monday morning because my entire staff was dancing around our conference table, pumping themselves up for our weekly kickoff meeting. And I know it was sunny because it was summertime in Los Angeles—the exorbitant property taxes ensure that the climate will never fall below a balmy seventy-three degrees.

We always dance it out before big meetings because it brings up our energy and gets us in the right headspace. Each week (to keep things fair) we rotate the role of house DJ, the person on our team who gets to pick our pump-up music. That summer, the entire staff (besides me) was under twenty-eight, so it was a millennial box of chocolates—you never knew what you were going to get. On that particular Monday I heard the song for the first time.

It was love at first listen.

If you've never rocked out to this particular piece, you should add it to your workout playlist immediately. It's upbeat and fun and irreverent to the point of challenge—the exact kind of inspiration you want before an intense cardio session or a first run in the local mayoral election.

Demi lets us know that she's looking great and feeling great and living her life on her own terms. And she's sorry, but she's not sorry. I live for this kind of jam. It's poppy and catchy and easily fits in the arsenal of music I use to give myself energy or alter my mood.

After that first experience, I quickly developed a song crush. I listened to it in the shower, at the gym, in the car—I even went so far as to play the Kidz Bop version when my children were around so I could keep it in rotation. I mean, that's commitment, you guys! Anyone who has ever suffered through Kidz Bop can attest that it's the seventh circle of parenting hell, but that's how much I loved this song. I listened to it all the time, and eventually a question popped into my head: *What am I not sorry about?*

See, Demi, she's not sorry about living life on her terms. She's not sorry for looking good or feeling good or making her ex-boyfriend jealous or taking a bubble bath in a Jacuzzi in the living room—if her music video is anything to go by. But what about me? What were the areas in my life that I absolutely refused to apologize for?

I wish I could tell you that every part of my life is a long list of not giving a tinker's damn what anyone else thinks, but that wouldn't be truthful no matter how much I want to set an example for you now.

As a sidenote, I spent much of my last Christmas holiday in bed sick with a horrible chest cold. I used that time to read many historical romance novels set in the Regency era with brooding dukes who were always saying things like, "Evangeline, I don't give a tinker's damn what society thinks!" just before kissing the heroine with the passion of ten thousand suns or whatever. My New Year's resolution was to start using the term *tinker's damn* in everyday speech. I've already accomplished my dreams, and it's only January 2. Huzzah!

But, truly, like many other women, I'm still in the process of overcoming a lifetime of people-pleasing. I constantly strive to move through every part of my life unconcerned with the opinions of others, but truthfully, I don't always achieve it. Yes, even me, the professional advice-giver, even I sometimes get trapped inside the crippling weight of other people's expectations and have to talk myself down from the ledge. But you better believe there are areas where I have mastered it. There are whole segments of my life where I've worked hard to keep my eyes on my own values and not worry what other people might think of them. The biggest example of this? Big, audacious dreaming. Massive, obnoxious goal setting. Being a proud working mother instead of buying into the special brand of oppression found inside mommy guilt. Daring to believe that I can change the world by helping women like you feel brave and proud and strong.

I may occasionally get tied up in the trappings of some stranger being mean on the internet about my hair or my clothes or my writing style—but I no longer spend a single second of my life worrying about what others think of me for having dreams for myself.

Embracing the idea that you can want things for yourself even if nobody else understands the whys behind them is the most freeing and powerful feeling in the world. You want to be a third-grade teacher? Wonderful! Open a dog-grooming studio where you specialize in dyeing poodles pink? Great! You want to save up to go on a lavish vacation where you ask everyone to refer to you as Bianca when your actual name is Pam? Fantastic!

Whatever the dream, it's yours, not mine. You don't have to give any justification, because as long you're not asking anyone to give you approval, then you don't need anyone to give you permission. In fact, when you understand that you don't have to justify your dreams to anyone else for any reason, that's the day you truly begin to step into who you're meant to be. I don't mean that you go around middle fingers up, like a Beyoncé song. I don't mean that you turn bitter and rude and shove your goals into other people's faces to prove a point. I mean that you focus in on the dream you have, you do the work, you put in the hours, and you stop feeling guilty about it!

Sadly, most people will go through their entire lives never experiencing that at all. Women especially are so brutal on themselves, and they often talk themselves out of their own dreams before they even attempt them.

This is a travesty.

There is so much untapped potential inside people who are too afraid to give themselves a chance. Right now there are women reading these lines who have ideas for nonprofits that would change the world . . . if only they had the courage to pursue their dreams. There are women reading these lines who have the potential to build a company that would alter their families' lives—and the lives of others who'd be positively affected by the business they created—if only they had the audacity to believe it would work. Right now there are women reading these lines who would invent the next great app, design the next great fashion line, write the next great bestselling book, or create the beauty products we'd all be obsessed with, if only they believed in themselves.

A dream always starts with a question, and the question is always some form of *What if* . . .

What if I went back to school?
What if I tried to build that?
What if I pushed myself to run 26.2 miles?
What if I moved to a new city?
What if I'm the one who could change the system?
What if God put this on my heart for a reason?
What if I could add some income to our bank account?
What if I could write a book that would help people?

That *what if*? That's your potential knocking on the door of your heart and begging it to find the courage to override all the fear in your head. That *what if* is there for a reason. That *what if* is your guidepost. That *what if* tells you where to focus next.

If every woman who heard that *what if* in her heart allowed it to feed the flame in her belly to pursue who she might be, not only would she shock herself with what she's capable of, but she'd astound everyone else as well. I'm convinced that if she—if we—just lived life in pursuit of answering that question, the effect on the world around us would be atomic.

Scientists estimate that we use only 10 percent of our brains. But have you ever seen one of those movies where the protagonist suddenly has access to all of it? They take a pill or get trained by a secret government agency, and all of a sudden they can bend metal with their minds and solve the world's poverty crisis in just a few hours because they're using their full potential. I'm convinced that many women in this world of ours are like Peter Parker, pre-radioactive spider bite—they're operating at a fraction of their potential because they haven't encountered a catalyst strong enough to unlock it.

Only a small part of our population is encouraged to believe in themselves and their potential from childhood on. People raised with advantages tend to see more possibilities. People who were taught self-worth from a young age are more likely to believe in their capabilities as adults. People with more resources usually perceive a goal as more easily achieved than those who have less. But what if you weren't raised to believe in yourself? What if you didn't have advantages or many resources? How likely would you be to believe you're capable of so much more? How likely would you be to stick with your goal when you get knocked off course?

But what if you did stick with it? What if you did believe? And not only you, but what if all sorts of women all over the world made the decision to replace other people's expectations with their own imaginations of who they might be?

Can you imagine if 25 percent more of the world, or 15 percent more or even just 5 percent more women decided to embrace their *what if*? Can you imagine if they stopped allowing the guilt or shame that comes from not being a certain way or a certain type of woman to squash their potential? Can you imagine the exponential growth we'd see in everything from art to science to technology to literature? Can you imagine how much more joyful and fulfilled those women would be? Can you imagine how their families would be affected? How about the community? How about other women who see their success and are inspired and emboldened by it and use it as a catalyst to spark change in their own lives? If that sort of revolution were to occur—a revolution of *what if*—we would change the world.

In fact, I believe we *can* change the world. But first, we've got to stop living in fear of being judged for who we are.

———

I've been sitting here for the last twelve minutes trying to figure out exactly how to ease us into this discussion topic, but you know what? We're all grown-up women; we can handle it. We can handle real conversation. We can handle someone holding a mirror up to our lives, and we can admit some hard truths when it comes to what's holding us back.

So here it is: women are afraid of themselves.

No, it's true. If we weren't afraid of ourselves we wouldn't spend so much time apologizing constantly for who we are, what we want out of life, and the time required for us to pursue both.

For the average woman, the story goes something like this. When you came into the world you were totally and utterly yourself. It wasn't a conscious decision to be exactly who you were; it was instinct. Were you loud? Were you quiet? Did you crave cuddles? Were you fine on your own?

Your needs were simple, your focus was crystal clear, and you didn't ever think about being any certain way—you just were. Then something changed. Something big happened, something that would shape the rest of your life, even if you couldn't have been aware of it at the time.

You learned about expectation.

There you were, being your adorable baby self, and suddenly that didn't cut it anymore. You were expected to do things: stop throwing your sippy cup on the floor, stop screaming when you don't get your way, start using the restroom like an actual person, stop biting your brother just because you feel like it. Two really critical things happened during the period when we switched from being totally accepted as is to having to live up to some expectation.

The first is that we learned to live within societal norms. This is a good thing because, sister, if you were still using a diaper at thirty-two because nobody helped you figure out a toilet, that would not be cute.

The second thing that happened is that we learned how to get attention, and to a child attention equals love. In fact, if you never learn any better, you'll go through your entire life believing that to have someone's notice means you are loved. See: social media as a whole.

Listen up, because I'm about to tell you something that may help you understand literally every person you know and possibly yourself as well. When you were a newborn you needed constant care and notice to stay alive, but at some point you stopped getting that undivided attention because you didn't need it anymore. But you still liked other people's regard (you were a baby after all), and so your clever mind started to test out ways to get notice on demand. Some toddlers get attention by being affectionate, so they learn to be dependent upon it. Some toddlers get attention by doing something that makes their parents laugh, so they learn to entertain. Some toddlers learn to get attention by doing something good that everybody praises; they become an achiever. Some toddlers notice that when they fall down and hurt themselves or when they're sick, Mommy gives them extra time and care; a hypochondriac is born. Some toddlers can't get any attention no matter what they do, so they kick and scream and throw a fit. Being angry is better than being ignored. These toddler tendencies can turn into childhood habits. Childhood habits that go unaltered turn into our unconscious ways of being.

I know it sounds like one big sweeping generalization, but seriously, ask yourself if this sounds like any adults you know. Do you have anyone in your life who always has problems? No matter what day of the week it is, the sky is always falling? That's because their problems give them the attention they crave from others. Do you know anyone in your life who's an overachiever? A workaholic? Always pushing themselves? That's likely because they—like me— got attention through achievement as a child, and the habit is hard to break. Do you know any women who seem utterly helpless? They constantly need someone else to help them, fix the problem, or counsel them through every decision? I'd bet my bottom dollar it's because they were raised in a home that fed them those lies or controlled every decision for so long that they have no confidence in their own capabilities.

My point is, we learn at a very early age that there are things we can do to hold on to attention, and even if the specifics of how we do it morph and change over time, the overarching way we're taught to gain notice as a child—from being entertaining to being an achiever, chronically sick, overly angry, or always in crisis—often remains the same and affects the way we seek attention as adults.

For me, it was always through achievement that I was able to receive notice from my parents. What this taught me at a very early age was that in order to be loved I needed to do things to earn it. Did my parents love me? Absolutely. But to a child for whom notice is the outpouring of love, the absence of any leads to a desperation to learn what she can do to receive it.

So, let's recap. You're a child and you learn that certain behaviors will get you notice. This begins to implant itself into who you're growing to become. But that's not the only hurtful thing you're learning. It's around the same age when you not only learn how to get love, but you're told *who you'll have to be* in order to keep receiving it.

Have you ever considered how much of your current life is truly made up of your choices and which areas are really just the things that were expected of you?

I was raised knowing that I would get married and have children . . . and quickly. In my small hometown, most of the girls I went to high school with had their first child by the time they were nineteen. When I had my first son at twenty-four I was practically ancient.

Twenty. Four.

What in the actual world? In retrospect that seems incredibly young to me. The idea of one of my kids having a baby by twenty-four makes me start to hyperventilate. There's so much life to live, so many things to see, so much you don't know about yourself yet at that age. I can't say that I'd change anything about when I got married or when I had babies, because that would mean I wouldn't have the children I have now. But the older I get the more I become aware that I was raised thinking that my real value was based on the role I would play for other people. After all, being deemed a good wife or a good mother or daughter is rarely based on how true you are to yourself.

Nobody is standing around after church on Sunday saying, "There goes Becca. You know she's devoted to self-care. What a good mama." Or, "Oh, look! Tiffany is training for her next half marathon. Look at all those hours she's putting into getting strong. What a good wife!" If those conversations are happening, it's nowhere near where I grew up. No, where I was raised women are taught that to be a good woman you need to be good for other people. If your kids are happy, then you're a good mom. If your husband is happy, you're a good wife. How about a good daughter, employee, sister, friend? All of your value is essentially wrapped up in other people's happiness. How can anyone successfully navigate that for a lifetime? How can anyone dream of more? How can anyone follow their *what if*, if they need someone else to approve of it first?

It's no wonder so many mothers send me notes telling me they've lost themselves. Of course they have! If you live your life to please everyone else, you forget what used to make you *you*. And what if you haven't found your partner yet or don't have a desire for children? Are you just a waste of a woman because there's no one else for you to be good for?

No. Of course not. You are a being with your own hopes and desires and goals and dreams. Some are little tiny ones ("I want to write poetry") and some are massive ("I want to create a million-dollar company"), but all of them are yours and they are valuable simply because you are valuable. You are allowed to want more for yourself for no other reason than because it makes your heart happy. You don't need anyone's permission, and you certainly shouldn't have to rely on anyone's support as the catalyst to get you there.

Unfortunately, many women struggle with what others might think of the goals they have for themselves. So instead of chasing them, they let their dreams die. Or they pursue them in secret or, worse, with a nagging sense of having failed those around them because they're doing something for themselves instead of everyone else. They live under guilt and shame and fear. *What if* stops being an ember of possibility in their hearts and becomes a litany of recriminations in their heads. *What if I fail? What if they laugh? What if I waste my time? What if this makes them mad? What if they think I'm greedy? What if I'm losing all this time with my family for nothing?*

When we stay in this place, fear runs our lives and prevents us from moving forward, even to the smallest degree. We may live with a massive fear of failure and a major perfectionist complex. Or we may be afraid because other people have already achieved what we're considering, so, what's the point? Or maybe we're afraid of embarrassment, of falling off the wagon (again). Or we worry we're not smart enough, pretty enough, young enough, old enough . . . so many possible ways we're not enough.

As women, we've had a lifetime of lies fueling our fears. We've had a lifetime of believing that our value lies primarily in our ability to make other people happy. We are afraid of so many things when it comes to our dreams, but the biggest fear is of being judged for having them in the first place.

I call BS.

It's about time someone did. I call BS to that lie in my own life, and I absolutely call it on your behalf as well.

At the beginning of every single year, I sit down and think of what the overarching theme will be for my work. I try to come up with a message for you, for my tribe, for this group of women that hangs out with me online. When I began writing this book, I asked myself what I wanted to say to you as women and sisters and daughters and friends and single ladies. What I wished you knew. And the answer that flowed out of my heart came from my *what if* spark.

If I could tell you anything, if I could convince you to believe it, it's that you were made for more. You were made to have the dreams you're afraid of having. You were made to do the things you don't think you're qualified for. You were made to be a leader. You were made to contribute. You were made to make changes for good, both in your local community and the world at large. You were made to be more than you are today and—this is the important part—your version of more might not look like my more, or hers.

For you, maybe *more* looks like finally signing up for the 10K. For someone else *more* might look like making strides to change the way she eats in order to be healthier. For someone else *more* might look like going back to school. For someone else *more* might look like getting out of the relationship with the person who is unkind and hurtful and cruel. *More* might look like not going back to the toxic relationship merry-go-round again and again and again. For someone else *more* might look like being kinder to herself. Maybe *more* is more time and rest. Maybe *more* is controlling your temper by counting to ten before you scream at your kids. Maybe *more* is getting in control of your emotions or *more* therapy or *more* water or *more* believing that you are capable of greatness or *more* not worrying what someone else thinks about you.

Made for more is the definition of you, and your desire for more is not something to be ashamed of! Our potential—the potential that resides in every single one of us—is our gift from our creator. What you do with that potential is your gift back to the rest of the world. The worst thing I can imagine is that you might die with that potential still untapped inside of you. And so I wrote this book, of the former Demi Lovato title, as encouragement, as a field guide, and also as the wind that fans the flames of your *what if* spark so that it turns into a wildfire.

Why?

Because the world needs your spark. The world needs your energy. The world needs you to show up for your life and take hold of your potential! We need your ideas. We need your love and care. We need your passion. We need your business models. We need to celebrate your successes. We need to watch you rise back up after your failures. We need to see your courage. We need to hear your *what if.* We need you to stop apologizing for being who you are and become who you were meant to be.

I spent a lot of time trying to figure out exactly how I wanted to lay out this book. It's the most—I hope anyway—tactical advice I've ever written down. I wanted it to be easy to understand and easy to apply to any kind of goal, and so I needed to get to the core of what has made it possible for me to achieve my dreams. What I finally asked myself was, *Which elements have either helped or hurt me in my pursuit of personal goals over the last fifteen years?* After all, I'm not an expert. I'm not a specialist or a professor, and I don't know the answer for everybody else. What I do know is how to get from a little town and a childhood filled with trauma to being a successful entrepreneur who built a multimillion-dollar company with only a high school diploma under her belt. I do know how to go from being an insecure young girl drowning in the anxiety of other people's perceptions to a confident and proud woman. I do know how to go from being severely overweight and unhealthy, using food as a coping mechanism and unable to walk up the stairs without getting winded to a marathon runner who leaps out of bed each morning ready to take on the day. I do know how to go from being a desperate people-pleaser just hoping for love to being a woman who is so filled with love for others, for my passions, for my work that I no longer need to seek it out in negative ways. All of these areas of growth in my life were once goals I had for myself, and while I didn't know what I was doing when I first started on this path, I can look back and see the commonalities between each success and failure that got me from there to here.

I am not an expert. What I am is your friend Rachel, and I want to tell you what worked for me. I have tried a bit of everything, but ultimately, achieving big goals both personally and professionally came down to these three things:

1. Letting go of the excuses that kept me stuck.
2. Adopting great habits and behaviors that set me up for success.

3. Acquiring the skills necessary to make exponential growth possible.

I honestly didn't have the self-awareness to identify these steps as I was living them, but I can look back now and see that these were the main factors that led to every success I've had along the way. I have laid each part of the book out in this foundational order on purpose.

I started with **excuses to let go of,** because if you don't recognize the things that are limiting you right now, you'll never be able to move past them. You'll notice, too, that the excuse section is the longest in this book. That's not an accident. The habits and skills we need are straightforward, but the litany of excuses that stand between where we are and where we want to go is longer and more dramatic than the second half of *Hamilton.* Once you wade through them and identify them as the lies they really are, you can move on to things that make you stronger.

The second part of this book is **behaviors to adopt,** which is my fancy way of telling you that your habits matter a great deal. If you want to see traction and results, consistency is key. Meaning, you can't just do something one time or even ten times and expect it to get you where you want to go. You have to develop behaviors that are so habitual they feel grounded in your DNA. You have to make it so living as the best version of yourself becomes your new normal.

Finally, I finish with **skills to acquire.** These are universal things everyone needs when pursuing any goal. What may throw you off is that these items are rarely listed out as skills. Things like confidence or persistence are typically considered characteristics you either have or you don't, but I want to change your perception about these things. You can cultivate new positive characteristics in yourself, and more importantly, you must if you want to achieve your personal goals more easily.

This book has a lot of information (it took me a lifetime to acquire it), but please don't allow that to overwhelm you. You are strong and bold and capable of more. From here on out, choose to see ideas for change as possibilities in your life. A life filled with possibilities is a recipe for your kind of greatness. Let's dive in!

PART I
EXCUSES TO LET GO OF

ex·cuse[1]

ik'skyo͞oz/

verb

1. attempt to lessen the blame attaching to (a fault or offense);
   seek to defend or justify.
2. release (someone) from a duty or requirement.
   synonyms: justify, defend, condone, vindicate

Excuses disguise themselves as any number of things.
Some people believe them with all their hearts. They really do
think they're not enough or that they don't have time or that
they're not a "goal kind of person." They don't realize that every
time they hold on to these beliefs, not only do they rob themselves
of motivation—they give up before they even start. Let's stop
doing that. What are the excuses you've been believing? Chances
are, one or more of these ideas has lived inside your head as justification for why you're not able to pursue and chase your dreams. I
hope that by digging into what the most common excuses are and
why we don't actually have to give them any power, you'll be able
to break the shackles currently holding you back.

EXCUSE 1:

THAT'S NOT WHAT OTHER WOMEN DO

I used to have shark teeth.

No, truly. I was one of those unfortunate children whose baby teeth wouldn't give up the ghost. Rather than shuffle out the door like any self-respecting incisor, they held on for dear life. Simultaneously, my adult teeth were having none of it. They came barreling into town like an aggressive in-law and took up residency. I had two rows of teeth. Shark teeth.

Around this same time, I decided to cut my own bangs with my dad's mustache scissors. Now, to give myself a little credit, I *did* recognize that this wasn't the smartest course of action. I was—and still am—a stringent rule follower, and cutting my own hair at age eleven was on par with performing open-heart surgery with Mema's mismatched silverware. Not advisable. But in this instance the bangs were hanging in my eyes and driving me crazy. As much as I was a rule follower, I was also—and still am—a woman of action. I decided to handle it myself. When my dad discovered the results of my pro-action, he attempted to rectify the uneven bang line. Unfortunately, he wasn't any better at barbery than I was. And he has terrible OCD . . . which means he's a stickler for a straight line. He kept cutting my bangs shorter and shorter, trying to get the edge neat, until they were barely longer than an eyelash. My fifth-grade pictures were a sight to behold.

Did I mention that I shaved my eyebrows in those days too? I didn't know how to pluck them yet. I only knew that I didn't want a unibrow any longer, and sliding my big sister's razor down the middle of my forehead seemed like the right choice.

I was also chubby.

And I played fifth-chair clarinet.

I was awkward and my hair was frizzy, and I was always twice the size of the cheerleaders and dressed in Goodwill clothes that rarely fit at all. All I wanted in the whole world was to be popular and pretty and to fit in with everyone else. And I didn't stand a snowball's chance in hell.

When you're little you have no control over the way you look or what you have access to or whether you fit in with the crowd. But you're absolutely aware of what's missing, what's lacking, what *should* be there. All you have to do is look in the direction of the people who do seem to fit in, who do seem to have it all figured out, to see your lack. In a perfect world, right about the time you notice your differences, someone older and wiser comes along and teaches you to value your unique and innate weirdness. They walk with you and speak truth into your life and, maybe, show you the best way to keep your hair from looking like that one episode of *Friends* where Monica visited Barbados. In a perfect world, they'd encourage you to be yourself while also helping you figure out how to improve in the ways that grow your self-confidence.

But most of us didn't grow up in that perfect world.

Most of us grew up identifying from a very early age all the things that were wrong with us. We believed we were too fat, too ugly, too awkward to be loved and accepted without making some big changes. Some women handle it by sinking further and further into themselves. Other women handle it by rebelling. *The world doesn't like my weird? Fine! I'll be so hugely other that I'll repel you before you get close!* Or, if you're like me, you decide right around the time of the shark teeth and the inch-long bangs that being this awkward and weird and tragic looking, frankly, sucks. So you, in all your prepubescent glory, start paying attention to what other girls are doing, and, like that scene in *The Little Mermaid* where she gets super fired up about finally having a chance to walk on dry land, you decide you, too, are going to be part of their world. You are going to do whatever it takes: act, dress, look, and speak in a way that offers you the most acceptance.

It wasn't a fast process, but eventually I got braces and learned to flat iron my hair. And by the time I was in my midtwenties, I'd gotten very good at playing a part. In fact, I'd gotten so good at being just like every other woman that it didn't even occur to me to question whether I enjoyed the choices I was making. By the time I started wondering whether I liked the road I'd put myself on, I felt too far gone to turn back.

And so I lived a double life.

Not like "paralegal by day and sleeper cell/international spy by night." More like I used to live my life—very publicly, it's worth saying—pretending to be one kind of person when I was actually someone else entirely.

In the public eye and on every social media platform, I was a wife and a mother, an avid home cook and food lover, a DIY queen with a blog and a penchant for Facebook posts. Behind the scenes I was a working mother, an entrepreneur, and a hustler of the highest order.

I had an office.

I had a full-time staff of five.

I worked sixty-plus hours a week.

And here's the important part—I loved every second of it.

I loved every second of it, but I never mentioned any of it. Not publicly on social media. Not privately at family parties. Not at business functions for my husband or even business meetings with potential clients. I downplayed it all. I waved the truth away like I was batting at a fly. *Oh, it's just this little thing I do.* I buried every accomplishment and didn't admit my biggest dreams even to myself. I worried about what others might think of me. I worried what *you* might think of me if you knew what was really inside my heart.

The truth was, there were so many things I was dreaming of. I had ideas to share with the world about how women could change their mind-sets, their mental health, their self-esteem, and, yes, the way they color in their eyebrows (because that matters to me almost as much as all the rest combined). I figured if I could build enough of a platform I could speak to women all over the world, and I could encourage them and lift them up and make them laugh. I believed that if other people could fill social media feeds with cat videos and latte pictures and workout posts, then I could add motivational quotes and positive affirmations into the mix. I believed I could change my whole business with the idea. I believed I could change the world.

I mean, who says that?

I do. Now, anyway.

Would I have five years ago, or ten? Absolutely not. I kept these secret dreams locked up nice and tight where nobody could consider them weird or judge me for them, and where, by the way, they'd never truly see the light of day or have a chance to manifest. Talents and skills are like any other living thing—they can't grow in the dark.

Perhaps what I did doesn't make sense to you. If it seems an odd thing to hide from your dreams, I'm going to assume you've never worked in my industry . . . or had trolls rip apart your character within the boundaries of a Facebook post. Let me tell you, it takes incredibly thick skin to ignore the mean things people say on the internet and, like a callus, that thick skin only develops when it's been ripped open a few times and healed tougher than before.

It took me years to have the courage to speak openly about my dreams.

I first began blogging when I was four years into running a successful event-planning firm in Los Angeles, producing fancy parties and elaborate weddings on my own. I was utterly burned out. Million-dollar events are glamorous to attend, but they're brutal to produce. At the end of my fourth year I was unsure whether I wanted to continue, but I had started this blog. At the time, blogging was exploding and everyone and their mother was into it, so I decided to try.

It was atrocious.

I literally wrote about what I ate for dinner the night before. My pictures looked like I had shot them in a dark room with a disposable camera—which wasn't far from the truth—and, honestly, nobody cared to read it. Like almost every part of my entrepreneurial career, I had no idea what I was doing. But, sister, let me tell you right now, in the absence of experience or knowledge, determination makes the difference between where you are and where you want to be!

As I started to narrow my focus and get more consistent with my content, a theme for my blog—and ultimately my business—began to emerge. I wanted to focus on the pursuit of a more beautiful life and a happier existence. I started to gain a small following and garner some attention. Then I received a few offers.

Could I talk about decorating for Thanksgiving on the local morning news? Of course I could! *Would I consider incorporating this brand of eggs into a recipe on my site for $250?* You're darn right, I would! *Could I wear those shoes in an upcoming Instagram post in exchange for a $100 Visa gift card?* Absolutely!

The offers came in steadily, and even though they were nowhere near what I was making as an event planner, there was gold in them there hills! Brands had money to spend, and they were looking to spend it with people like me. Slowly but surely, over the next nineteen months, I grew the revenue stream for the blog and took on fewer and fewer event clients until I could make the transition completely. By then I had scaled back to a part-time intern as my only source of help, and when I decided to focus on the blog completely, I knew I needed some professionals. My goals for myself have always been lofty, even if I didn't feel comfortable telling people what they were. I have no idea how to play small at anything. An excessive imagination plus a lifelong desire to prove my worth through achievement means I'm always aiming for the sun.

You know that expression "Go big or go home"? I never go home.

If you give me a wiener dog puppy for my birthday, I'm going to . . . well, number one, I'm going to be surprised. I've never asked for a wiener dog so I'm not sure what this gift even means, but I'll embrace it wholeheartedly. I'll name him something elegant, like Reginald Wadsworth, the eighth Duke of Hartford, and it won't be long until I'm imagining building a small farm outside Phoenix where I can raise my championship dachshunds for competition.

The point is . . .

As soon as I decided to grow the blog side of the business, I knew I needed staff to help me do it. I hired editors to help me write and photographers to take gorgeous photos and an assistant to run my office. As our content grew, so did the fan base. We worked hard and paid attention to trends, and as the audience grew so did the revenue. It was fantastic. It was a company built on my reputation and, ultimately, the ideal that these fans had created about me.

Allow me to take a side step here and explain something about celebrities or social influencers that I didn't understand at the time. Right now, while I'm writing this book, I have just over a million fans on social media. But at that earlier point in my business history I probably had ten thousand fans on Facebook, and Instagram didn't exist yet. Regardless, the deal with any sort of fame is just as true today as it was back then, and here it is: You don't know me. You only know your perception of me. The same is true for The Rock or Oprah or a Kardashian or the president. Even when someone is as transparent as possible—and I would argue that, between pictures of my stretch marks going viral and my last book where I admitted everything from abusing alcohol to being bad at sex, I lead a very transparent public life—even then you don't know the actual person. Not because they're necessarily secretive, but because you perceive them through the lens you've created.

So, for instance, if you first started following me on Instagram because of a picture of me looking extra stylish, you might think of me as stylish and on-trend. If you came on board during the aforementioned stretch-marks photo explosion, then you might identify with me as a mother or someone who has battled with body-image issues. Whatever you perceive about me (or anyone you don't truly know) has way more to do with the box you've put us in than who we actually are. This is all totally natural and fine, unless that person you admire steps outside the lane you put them into.

For me, that lane was motherhood. And here's where the whole double-life thing I mentioned earlier comes into play.

I had a legion of fans who were moms (and I still do to this day), but at the time I hadn't publicly talked about my company. It wasn't that I was ashamed; I was simply so focused on creating content that I never stopped to explain how it had all come into the world. I assumed everyone would realize I must have had help. I was creating six intricately produced blog posts every single week, and I had two small children. Of course I had help! But for whatever reason, that wasn't apparent to most people, and when they realized the truth, some of them were pissed. And ruthless. I don't even recall what it was for, but I know it was a Facebook post where I talked about being a mom. In the comments someone asked when I had time to "do it all." It didn't even occur to me to lie.

"Oh, I don't do it all," I blithely typed back. "My husband is really involved, and we have a nanny who helps with the boys while I'm at work."

The internet exploded.

"What kind of mother lets someone else raise her children?"

"Only a selfish bitch would choose work over family!"

"Must be nice to lay around all day while some other woman raises your kids."

The vitriol was immediate and intense. Some fans were disheartened to learn that I had help in producing the content. Many women were very upset that I had a job outside the home. Others were apoplectic that I had a nanny. I can understand in retrospect that they had perceived me to be a stay-at-home mom, likely because that's who they were. We tend to see people not as they are but as we are. When I stepped outside the lane they had built for me, they felt cheated or lied to.

I was devastated.

I could not handle that people were so upset with me. Never

mind that they were absolute strangers. Never mind that it was in the comments of a Facebook post. I was gutted. Remember little girl me? Remember Shark Teeth? Well, she still desperately wanted to belong, and she hated the idea that anyone might be upset with her.

It honestly seems stupid in retrospect, because I'm so far removed from that insecure young woman (thank you, therapy!). But it made me second-guess everything I did and said publicly. There were a handful of topics I knew would make people angry, so I stopped mentioning them altogether. Working, entrepreneurialism, my team, having a nanny, having a housekeeper, business trips—it all quickly became taboo. I focused on what people loved. Pinterest-worthy photos on how to get organized, parenting advice, exercise tips, and cupcake recipes ruled the day. I worked my butt off for years to grow and scale my company, but if you asked me at the time what I did for a living, I would demurely tell you that I had "a little blog."

That "little blog" was read by millions of people every month and had a six-figure revenue stream, but I understood that the business behind the blog was upsetting to certain people, so I never mentioned it. And it wasn't like I just kept certain aspects of my life quiet. The very nature of keeping it a secret started to reinforce the idea that what I was doing—and who I was—was something to be ashamed of. This fed my mommy guilt. This fed my insecurities about the right way to be a wife. When anyone said anything negative about my choices, either online or in person at a family function, I didn't question it. I came to believe that they were right, that I was doing all this wrong, that a good woman or wife or mother would live totally for her family.

Only I couldn't give it up. I loved my business, and I loved trying to solve the puzzle of entrepreneurship. It made me happy. It lit my heart on fire. It made me feel alive. But, simultaneously, I didn't want anyone to be inconvenienced by the thing that gave me joy.

How many of you do that? How many of you reading this are living half lives or, worse, are a shadow of who you were truly meant to be because someone in your life doesn't fully appreciate or understand you?

I didn't want to give up on my dream of a successful business, but I also didn't want anyone to disapprove of me. I lived this double life for nearly five years and suffered from constant anxiety attacks. It took a ton of personal work and some big realizations for me to get to the root of why I felt the need to live this way, but the gist of it is this: I cared more about being loved by others than I cared about loving myself.

So while I continued growing my business, I stopped mentioning it publicly. And when members of our family questioned why I would work rather than stay at home with our children—constantly and with increasing frustration—I learned not to mention it privately either.

Brené Brown says, "Shame is a focus on self, guilt is a focus on behavior. . . . Guilt: I'm sorry. I made a mistake. Shame: I'm sorry. I am a mistake."[1] I didn't understand it at the time, but I felt extremely ashamed of being a working mom. And I felt ashamed for years. Years of beating myself up, years of trying to please everyone else, years of trying to be exceptional at producing family dinners and toddler birthday party designs in order to prove that my children weren't missing out on anything. So many years I wasted knotted up inside about other people's expectations for my life. So many years being distracted from my core mission to motivate and help other women, because I was so worried about everyone else's perception.

So many years I spent apologizing for who I was.

Oh, not verbally apologizing. My apologies were so much more hurtful because I didn't say I'm sorry with my words. I apologized with the way I lived my life. Every time I felt ashamed for taking a business trip. Every time I swallowed the lie of mommy guilt. Every time I dressed a certain way or spoke a certain way in order to be better received was an apology for who I really was, a lie of omission. And every single time I lied about who I was, I reinforced the belief in my own mind that there was something wrong with me. I honestly believed I was the only woman who felt this way.

Then, in 2015, I went to a conference that would change my life forever. I talked about it in detail in my last book, and I swear I won't be that author who just repeats all her old stories in the sequel, but the gist of that experience was, we were doing some work on limiting beliefs and the lies that hold us back. I began to dig into my childhood and what I might have learned or accepted back then that was still affecting me today.

Spoiler alert: most of the things you learned in childhood are still affecting you today. I was no exception.

I grew up in a home with a traditional structure. Dad worked, and Mom took care of the house . . . even when she also worked. Somehow I still found my way into being a proud feminist—which means, in its totality, that I believe men and women should be treated equally. I went into marriage believing my husband and I would equally share the load, but it was so easy to slip back into the structure I'd grown up with that told me what a woman should be like and how she should act and what her value was.

Let me step to the side for a moment and unpack the idea of living into what a "woman is supposed to be." If I only get to give you one thought to chew on in this book, it would be this: Most of us have been raised with a massive disparity between the way women should be and the way men should be. This isn't a question of masculine versus feminine. I'm typing this out right now while wearing full makeup—with contouring! This is a question of who little boys are raised to be versus who little girls are raised to be. Like I mentioned earlier, most women, regardless of where they grew up or what their cultural background is, have been taught essentially that to be a good woman is to be good for other people. The problem with this is that it means you're letting other people determine your worth. Is it any wonder that half the women I know suffer from anxiety and depression, drowning underneath the wave of what other people think? We've been taught that we don't have any value without the good opinions of others.

But I digress. I went to this conference and had a life-changing epiphany. I had been taught to play small, but I had been born with a heart that only dreamed big. That heart and all it encompassed had been built into me while I was still forming. My dreams weren't just a part of me; they were the core of who I was. They were a gift from God, and if my creator endowed me with something, how could it be wrong? I dug deeper and realized that my desire for growth and work only really felt wrong when I started to worry what other people might think of it. Staying at home can be a beautiful personal choice and life calling—but it wasn't mine. It was what other people wanted for my life. It was culturally what we knew, but that didn't make it right for me. So I started to wonder, *What if what was right was truly believing in myself enough to be honest about my life? What if what was right was being proud of who I was made to be? What if what was right was to find pride in my hard work and accomplishments and to stop playing small?*

I left that conference on fire! I came home a completely different woman—or actually, I should say, I came home fully living into myself for the first time in my life. The years since then have been the happiest, most fulfilled, and most rewarding of my entire

existence, and they've also made me aware of something important. I didn't corner the market on feeling ashamed because I didn't
fit into the mold of the other women around me. I'm not the only
one who has ever carried around those feelings. But the catalyst
that propelled me into the dreams I'm so privileged to be living
today is that I accepted the challenge to actively get past those feelings and, in doing so, massively changed my life.

If you've been affected by my work, if you enjoyed the last
book or had a life-changing weekend at one of our conferences or
found nuggets of wisdom in my podcast, remember that none of
that would have happened if I hadn't stopped listening to that little
voice inside my head that says, "This is not what other women
are like. This is too bold, too weird, too obnoxious. Sit down. Be
quiet." Fighting the instinct to listen to that voice is one of the
hardest things I've ever worked through, but because I did, my
life—and maybe yours too?—changed for the better.

EXCUSE 2:

I'M NOT A GOAL-ORIENTED PERSON

My instinct is that the majority of the women who pick up this book are goal diggers. Not gold diggers—goal diggers. Meaning, you have a goal or a dream that's been on your heart and you want some advice or encouragement to propel you forward. But chances are, amongst the crowd are also women who are curious or wondering or maybe just fans of my YouTube channel who aren't really sure how this whole goal thing is going to work for them, because, well, they're just not a goal-oriented kind of gal. They've decided that it's simply their genetic makeup; some people are into that whole "personal growth thing" and some people aren't. These people may even wish they were that kind of person but don't have a lot of hope for it, because "that's just not the way I'm wired."

The thing is, I totally understand why you'd think that. I mean, obviously if you didn't come into the world already having mastered something, it was just never meant to be yours. Walking, speaking, eating solid foods without choking to death, driving a car, spelling, using a computer—all of that was just naturally a part of "who you were" from birth, right?

No. Don't be dumb!

You learned those skills just like you learned a million other things. I'm not arguing that you aren't currently a goal-oriented person, because perception is reality and if you believe it's true then it absolutely is. What I'm arguing is that you're missing a word in the sentence. You're not a goal-oriented person *yet*. Finding your goal, focusing in on it, and learning to work to get closer to it every day is possible for anyone. Finding your goal takes some soul-searching and some clarity, but the other two? Having focus and being productive enough to get closer to where you want to go? Those are just habits. If you don't already have them, it's only because you haven't developed them yet. Not because they'll never be yours.

Dreams are things you hope for, for your life. Dreams are the things that occur to you as you go about your day. Things like, *I wish I didn't feel so tired all the time. Wouldn't it be great to get into shape?* Or, *I'd love to be debt-free.* Or, *I wish we could take a luxury vacation this summer.* Or, *I wish we didn't have to live paycheck to paycheck. Maybe I could start a side business.* Because we all come from different places and backgrounds, our dreams are as unique and varied as our hairstyles. Everyone has dreams for their life—everyone. Not everyone admits it to themselves or even considers their idle wishes a possibility, but every single person reading this book wants something. Those wishes you have? Those are dreams. But a dream and a goal are two different things entirely.

A goal is a dream with its work boots on. A goal is a dream you've decided to make real. A goal is a destination you're working toward instead of an idea you're only considering or hoping for. Hope is a beautiful thing and an incredibly valuable tool to help keep us motivated and inspired about the possibility for the future. But let's be very clear on this point: hope is not a strategy.

Simply hoping that life will get better, that you'll get better, that you'll suddenly develop focus and motivation when you're not taking any active steps to make that a reality, is worthless. You've got to plan for your success. You've got to be intentional, and you've got to decide right now that you can be whoever you want to be and achieve whatever you want to achieve.

You've got to believe it.

You've got to believe in yourself and believe that you're capable of making changes to become whatever kind of person you want to be. As you read through this book, as you're trying to figure out the person you want to be, remember the journey starts with the goal. It starts with finding the direction you want to go in and then figuring out how to build the habits that will get you there.

Truly one of the best moments of my career in the last five years was a phone call I had with a member of our community. This group is made up of millions of women all over the world (and a few good men) who hang out with us on social media. We were on with one of our members, asking her about her experience attending our first conference. The very first year we put on the Rise conference, we truly had no idea what we were doing. I only knew that I wanted to create an opportunity for women to come together and hear wisdom and ideas that would give them the tools to change their lives, while also providing an opportunity for them to hang out with a community of like-minded women. So we were on a call with one of the women who was brave enough to come to our first event to hear about her experience. On the call this woman mentioned sheepishly that she only went to the conference because she was hoping I would sign her copies of my fiction books. She'd never focused on personal growth before.

"I never knew I could have a goal," she told us. "I'm a mom and a wife, and I never thought about focusing in on something just for me."

To be totally honest, I was stunned by this revelation. Stunned because, well, I am a very goal-oriented person (as if you couldn't tell) and it had honestly never occurred to me that not everyone was. Oh, sure, I get that not everybody leaps out of bed at 5:00 a.m. like a jack-in-the-box as I do, but I just assumed that everybody was always working toward something. And the fact that someone could come to one of our events and leave understanding that she as a woman had value for herself, not for what she could provide to other people—not for her kids, not for her husband, not for her mom, but for herself—was eye-opening to me. She discovered that she was allowed to have a dream and a desire and a goal, and, holy crap, that was amazing, and it made me so proud of our company.

But it also served as a lesson to me and made me understand that there are those of you who don't allow yourselves a goal or even a dream. It makes my heart ache. Not because I'm over-dramatic (though I am that most definitely) but because growth is happiness. Truly. Having something to work toward gives us purpose. Achieving new milestones, even little ones, gives us a sense of accomplishment and pride. All living organisms, relationships, and businesses are either growing or they're dying. Period.

If you find yourself going through life without anything to work toward or aim for, it's no wonder that you feel like your life is living you instead of the other way around. I don't care if you're the CEO of a Fortune 500 company or a stay-at-home mom—you've got to have a goal. It can be a personal goal you set for yourself to get in shape or save money or own a home or build a business or save your marriage. It can be anything at all. Just know that you're supposed to have one, and even if you've never been able to focus in on one before, you can develop the habit and you can become the kind of person who is, well, any damn thing she wants to be.

EXCUSE 3:

I DON'T HAVE TIME

I'm going to assume that lack of time is something every single person reading this book can identify with. Maybe you're a single parent. Maybe you're a recent college grad working two jobs to survive. Maybe you're an empty nester with a full schedule. The truth is, no matter where you are or which season of life you're in, there's a solid chance that you struggle to find time. Often there doesn't seem to be time for the things you'd like to have more of in life: time with your friends, time with your partner, time to get a massage or walk through Target alone for a whole hour without your kids just so you can remember what it's like to shop slowly and hands-free. But it can also be hard to find time for your goal. When are you going to pursue it? Where will you fit it in with your current job or your current life or the current children you have to keep alive? How can you add this to a schedule that already feels overwhelming and too big to carry?

Well, sister, here's the truth, and it may or may not surprise you that I've given this answer before, but it remains true. You aren't going to find the time to pursue your goals; you're going to make the time to pursue your goals. And the first thing you're going to need to accept is that you are in control of your schedule. Yes, you, high-level executive. Yes, you, mama of four. Yes, you, college student with twenty-seven events this week. Yes, you, entry-level assistant with a demanding boss. You are in control of your schedule. In fact, there isn't one thing in your life or your calendar right now that you didn't allow to be there. Let that sink in for a second. Being overscheduled? That's on you. Not finding time to feed yourself? You. Spending two hours a night watching TV or scrolling Instagram as a way to relax? Also your choice.

Girl, the question is never, Do you have enough time? The question is, How are you using the time you have? It's possible to put yourself through college while being a stay-at-home mom. Women do it all the time. It's possible to train for a half marathon while working full-time. Women do it all the time. It's possible to build your own business at night after you finish working at someone else's company. I did it.

Back when I was still a coordinator working in the entertainment industry, I started to fantasize about what it would be like to own my own company. I dreamed about it endlessly, and in the days before Pinterest I would tear pictures from magazines and store them in a binder for someday. At the time I worked fifty-plus hours a week at my day job and I had been married less than a year, so there were plenty of things to fill up my weekends. It was fun to watch marathons of Drew Barrymore movies on TBS. It was fun to go to the Home Depot and try to remodel our powder room. It was fun to save up for the Wagon Wheel Sampler Platter at the Black Angus on date night. And, after working all week long, there were few things more enjoyable than hanging out with Dave at home. But as the dream of starting an event-planning company began to grow bigger and bigger in my heart, I knew I'd have to give up something. Quitting my job and going solo as a new business owner just wasn't possible. We had a little townhouse with a big mortgage that needed to be paid—it took both our salaries to make that happen. I didn't have the money to go out on my own. I didn't have connections or a mentor or potential clients or a hefty savings account. All I had was time and—and here's the key—a willingness to trade that time in pursuit of what I wanted.

That's how life works.

It's been said that, "If you want something you've never had, you have to do something you've never done." For me, that meant I gave up weeknights watching TV with my new husband. I gave up my weekends wandering around Bed Bath & Beyond to find a new duvet for the guest room. Instead, I worked. I interned for local wedding planners so I could learn the industry. I traded hundreds of hours on my feet *in heels* at weddings and movie premieres for knowledge of how I might be able to do this on my own. I worked for a solid year in one of the hardest, most thankless jobs on the planet (event assistant at high-end parties), in addition to my regular working hours, and I worked them for free. I never got a nickel for those hours. I traded comfortable weekends at home with Dave for the opportunity to work with demanding clients and abusive event planners in order to learn about the industry I wanted to be a part of.

Not to put too fine a point on this, but it sucked! Do you think I wasn't tired after my regular job? Do you think I wanted to go run a wedding rehearsal for a bridezilla on a weeknight after putting in ten hours at the office? Do you think I wanted to miss out on friends' birthday parties and weekends away so I could work a wedding? Do you think it wasn't discouraging to be treated badly when I was working for free? Of course it was. But, dude, look where it got me!

I used the knowledge I learned that year to launch my own event-planning company. I used that event-planning company to start my blog. That blog gave me this fan base. And later, that year I spent working for mean-girl event planners gave me the story line for my first bestselling fiction book, *Party Girl*. Learning to carve time out of my day back when I first started in business meant that whenever I wanted to commit to something new, I understood that the only thing standing between me and my new goal was a willingness to find time for it.

For instance, when I wanted to write that first book, I started waking up at 5:00 a.m. in order to push toward my word count before my kids woke up. I learned to write whenever and how-ever I could in order to get to my goal. That tactic still serves me to this day. Right now, I'm editing this chapter on the stairs of an overcrowded gate at the Toronto airport. I've just spent three days doing press and book signings, and I'm exhausted to the marrow of my bones. But I believe in this book, and I want to get it into your hands as soon as possible, which means I'm choosing to sacrifice some rest time in order to make this happen. If I want to achieve any new thing in my life, the question is never, Can I do it? The question is always, What am I willing to give up in order to get it?

That's what it boils down to. Not whether or not you have the time, but whether this goal you have is so compelling, so beautiful, so *necessary* to your future happiness that you're willing to trade your current comfort in order to achieve it. You in? You willing to give up a little of today's rest for tomorrow's possibilities? The first step is to get over the excuse that you don't have the time. The next step is to reconfigure the time you do have in order to achieve the goal you're after. Here's how:

1. MAKE A TIMELINE OF YOUR CURRENT WEEK.

You know how, when you meet with a nutritionist for the first time, they ask you to keep a food diary for a week so you know every single thing you consume? This is the same idea. You need to account for every single hour in an average week. I want you to list out everything you do. The easiest way is to open a calendar app on your phone and document as you go. Did you go on a run that took forty-five minutes? Add it. Did you volunteer at the church bake sale? Add in all the time it took, including getting ready, drive time, et cetera. Did you spend fifty-eight hours this week playing Candy Land with your toddler? We all bow down . . . that's saint-hood work right there. Put it in the calendar.

Once you've recorded an entire week, figure out where you have the time to add five hours a week to work on your goal. Don't hyper-ventilate. Five hours is not actually that much time. That's one hour a day for five days out of seven. That's one three-hour session and less than a handful of thirty-minute segments. There are a ton of ways to mix and match this time. The point is that you decide right now that you're committing five hours a week minimum to your goal.

If you've hung out with me long enough, you know that I have some daily habits that help me live my best life, which I call "Five to Thrive." Well, sister, these five hours are goal based and have a fun name too: "Five to Strive." As in, you're going to commit to five hours a week striving for your goal, minimum. If you've got more time, give it, but at the very least, make a habit of your five hours and stick to it!

2. ONCE YOU'VE SET YOUR NEW SCHEDULE, TREAT YOUR "FIVE TO STRIVE" HOURS AS SACRED.

If I open your calendar next week, I should see a life that's set up around the things that you want to achieve. Let's say you told me, "My goal is to get into incredible shape this year because my hus-band and I have always wanted to run a half marathon together and this is our year." If I open your schedule right now, will I see three appointments a week to run?

When something is sacred you protect it. Imagine I came to you and said, "Hey, do you want to meet Chris Hemsworth for coffee at 3:00 p.m.?" You would of course say yes because he's dreamy and he has an accent and you're more than a little curious why Chris even knows who you are. You would put it in your calendar as a non-negotiable because there are so many awesome and exciting things you'll experience with that appointment in your calendar. Then, if all of a sudden someone said, "Hey, can you pick up the kids at 3:10? I know I said I was going to do it, but I can't now." You wouldn't just agree. You wouldn't just blithely blow off your date, because it's Chris-*freaking*-Hemsworth, and that scheduled appointment, that promise to yourself, is something you wouldn't give up lightly.

Whatever vision you have for your future, it has to be at least as valuable to you as that coffee date with Thor . . . or whoever your version of Thor is. You have to recognize that your commitment to it will yield just as many awesome and exciting things as a date with a hunky Australian superhero. These five hours are what's in between you and something great, and if you can't commit the time in your schedule to becoming the person that you want to be, what are we even doing here? Why are we even trying? Is your schedule populated by things that will make your life better, or is it dictated by everybody else's wants and needs?

3. MAKE SURE YOUR MINIMUM HOURS ARE YOUR BEST HOURS.

I write best and fastest in the morning. I'm more energized than I am later in the day, and I don't have decision fatigue that makes me overthink everything. I can write at night, but it feels like a slog and it typically takes me twice as long to get the exact same word count. I know this about myself, so I schedule my minimum hours for the mornings. It's not enough to simply make time for the hours; you have to also schedule them for when you've got the mental capacity to do them well.

4. PLAN YOUR SCHEDULE WEEKLY.

You have to. Every Saturday or Sunday, Dave and I sit down together and go through our calendars. We talk about work meetings, our kids' drop-off and pickup schedules, our workouts and the time we're planning to go out with friends, and our weekly date night. We also reaffirm our priorities so we both know what's on each other's plates and where we might need some extra support. Life happens, you guys, and your schedule will shift and change. Those sacred hours? They might have to show up at a different time or on a different day from week to week in order for them to make it into your schedule at all. If you wait until midweek to try and find a place for them, the chances are less likely you'll actually get to the thing you know you need to be doing. You can't just plan your calendar at the beginning of the month and expect it to stick; you're not an android. Schedule at the start of the month and again at the start of each week to make sure you adhere to the plan.

You can make the time to pursue your goals, and you have to do it now. Why now? Because if not now, then when?

I didn't use to wear makeup.

Well, I guess I did wear makeup, but not often and not well. My oldest sister, Christina, was and is a makeup aficionado. Her hair was big and blonde, and her eyeshadow was flawless. I should have followed suit, but she's nine years older than me, so I missed the boat on the whole tutorial thing. I suppose that explains why a quick swipe of mascara was the best I could come up with in my teenage years. And, unfortunately, acquiring hair or makeup skills is not something magically granted to you on your eighteenth birthday, like the ability to buy lottery tickets.

All of this to say that just because I was a legal adult didn't mean I was any closer to appearing pulled together. But necessity is the mother of invention, and as the years progressed I managed to work a "day face" into my routine. A bit of shadow, some liner, a little concealer, and a clear lip gloss became part of the uniform that I put on when I had to go into my office every day. But at night or on a weekend? No way! Makeup or curling my hair was for something special, like a date or a party. The rest of the time you could find me in yoga pants with my hair in a bun.

Then one day I was planning to meet some friends for dinner, and on my way past the bathroom mirror I had a moment of pause. I didn't look great, but I didn't want to fuss with getting ready. I thought, *Is having dinner with my girlfriends enough of a reason to take the time to do my makeup?* And almost immediately I answered my own question.

"If not now, then when?" I asked my ill-kempt reflection. I was living my entire life waiting for a moment to be special enough for me to look, feel, and act my best, and the truth is, you don't need a special moment, or any reason at all, to do that. If not now, then when? This saying became my mantra and the answer to a dozen different questions.

Should we eat off the nice wedding china or paper plates?

Should I dress up for a date with my husband or just wear
     jeans again?

Should I take the time to write a note to a friend?

Call Mema and Papa?

Bake some cookies for the neighbors?

The answers to all of these questions is the same: If not now, then when? You could spend forever planning out your someday when right now, today, this second, this is all you've got. Someday isn't guaranteed!

So stop waiting for someday; someday is a myth. Don't wait to have the time; start planning to make the time.

EXCUSE 4:

I'M NOT ENOUGH TO SUCCEED

I've talked a lot in my writings and my speaking about my lifelong battle with not feeling good enough. It is one of the topics I get the most notes about, so I know I'm not alone with those insecurities. For many of us, the list of not enough comes in every size and shape. We battle with feelings of lack in almost every major area of our lives. But it's a whole different ball game when we are setting out to achieve something we're unsure we can actually do.

The lack of enough in other areas of our lives is hard as it is. *I'm not pretty enough to find a spouse. I'm not thin enough to be beautiful. I'm not old enough to pursue that. I'm not young enough to pursue this.* We're already grappling with feeling like we're not enough simply in our existence, and now we've got to throw a goal out in front of us. Are the insecurities we feel about regular life supposed to be absent in this area? Of course not! In fact, when we set out to pursue something, we're often dealing with our fear of what we lack multiplied by a factor of nine million.

You think you're not fit enough in general, and now you're supposed to run a half marathon? You think you're not smart enough in school, but somehow you're going to build a successful business? You think you're not dedicated enough, but you're going to attempt writing a book? And so, what happens too often is that you subconsciously decide that you're going to fail before you ever even attempt to succeed. The irony, of course, is that the thing you're attempting to take on might be the exact thing that proves your misconceptions about yourself wrong. If you successfully run the half marathon, it would affect the way you feel about what your body is capable of. If you build an incredible business, it would adjust your beliefs about how smart you are. If you stick with it and finally finish that manuscript, it would prove that you are dedicated. It's a catch-22, because your feelings of *not enough* keep you from proving to yourself that you are. You haven't yet achieved the things you hope for, and so you decide that you're unable to.

Why do we treat only certain areas of our lives this way? When you fall down while trying to learn to walk as a toddler, you don't stay down. You get right back up and try again. The first time you drove a car, you were probably scared and nervous and holding on to the steering wheel with a kung-fu grip and a proper placement at ten and two. Nowadays you could likely steer with your left knee while handing a sippy cup to someone in the back seat without missing a single word of the *Dora the Explorer* soundtrack you've got on repeat for school drop-off. We fail and slip up and screw up and fall down over and over again in our youth, and yet we keep on going. But ask a thirty-seven-year-old woman to take up CrossFit for the first time, and she'll immediately start to imagine all the reasons she'll suck at it, and before she knows it, she's talked herself out of even trying a single time.

I think this is because the younger you are, the more failure is expected and the less aware you are of what other people might think if you fall. But, girl, the things you're attempting to do now aren't things that you've accomplished before, so they should get toddler status. It's not that you're not enough to cross the finish line; it's just that you haven't yet figured out how to run this particular race.

But I get it. This is something I have also struggled with. The thing that has hindered me from chasing down one of my biggest goals in life has been the belief that I'm not smart enough to build a big business. Or I guess I should say that I've felt like I'm not educated enough. When I admit that, it tends to surprise people, I suppose because I recognized this limiting belief years ago and have since worked hard to shift my perception of myself. You see, anytime we feel lacking, the only way to successfully fight back against that lie is with a truth that makes it irrelevant.

I'll admit that I am uneducated in the traditional sense. I have a high school diploma and one year of acting school. That's it. It wasn't an issue when I was an event planner, because people were hiring me for my skill with design and organization. Nobody cared about whether I had an MBA. But over the last handful of years my company has grown exponentially, and with that exponential growth has come more revenue and expenses, and you guys, I am freaking terrible at math. Because it's not an area I felt confident in, I did my best to ignore the financials of my business. The more revenue we brought in, the more I struggled to understand a balance sheet that suddenly resembled the budget intricacies of a small island nation. It became a self-fulfilling prophecy.

It pains me to admit this to you, but a couple of years into this process of building my company, I had barely looked at our books. They overwhelmed me, and I didn't understand what I was looking at. So I hardly even glanced at the financial reports our accountant would run for us. As long as I had enough money to cover payroll and clients were paying their bills on time, I didn't really pay attention. Truthfully, it wasn't laziness or complacency that was driving this decision. It was fear. Every time I looked at a financial statement and didn't understand it, that voice in my head—you know the one, that jerk version of yourself that likes to point out all your flaws—would list out all the things I was deeply worried about. *You're not smart enough to run a company at this level. Who do you think you are? These people are trusting you with their livelihoods, and you can't even read a balance sheet. You're going to fail.* This fear and this circle of self-recrimination went on for years, and then one day I just got sick of it.

I was reading an excellent book on sales, and I was super fired up about all these ideas I was gathering about growing our revenue and lowering our overhead. But in order to do those things, I understood that I had to—absolutely had to—get a handle on where we were financially. Immediately the fears started to creep in, but my excitement over where I wanted to go was greater than my fear. My loud Okie family has a saying, and that morning, as I was sitting at my desk, it popped into my head.

"Rach," I said out loud to myself. "Either piss or get off the pot."

Crude? Absolutely. But sometimes you need to hear your grandpa's straightforward, no-nonsense voice in your head to remind you of who you really are. I was either going to run this business and scale it with courage and determination and faith in myself, or I needed to stop playing at it. My limiting belief was that I wasn't smart enough because I lacked an education in business finances to help me understand. I needed to counteract this limiting belief with a truth that took away its power.

The truth I reminded myself of was that I had always figured things out in the past. Always. I'd owned my own company for fourteen years and had never one time shrunk from a challenge. So what? Now that I was actually becoming successful on a large scale, I was suddenly going to give up? Just because I was unsure? No way! As I started to pump myself up with this truth, I got enough clarity to ask myself a better question. Instead of accepting that I wasn't smart enough, I worked the specific problem in front of me. How could I better understand this? Was there a class I could take?

Of course there was! I immediately applied for and got accepted to an online business accounting program through Harvard Business School. The idea, of course, was that if I felt I wasn't smart enough, the antidote to that must be applying for one of the most difficult online programs available for me that day. Once I passed that class, I told myself, that would prove to me—nay, to the world!—that I was good at numbers. A psychologist would have a field day.

Taking that class was an abysmal failure.

For one thing, it was freaking expensive. For another, I aced my tests and pulled good grades, but it was only because I studied and tested well. Once it was over, I truly had no greater knowledge about any of the concepts than I did when I started. Also, it was hugely time-consuming, which actually made me way more anxious about successfully leading my company, because I was spending a good chunk of my day on schoolwork.

I'm telling you this part of the story because I think it's a pitfall that many of us make on the road to personal growth of any kind. We identify the problem. We decide that we're going to fix it. We attempt to fix our personal problem by doing something that in no way resembles us personally.

It's like Sara deciding she's going to get in shape and signing up for a series of crazy-expensive SoulCycle classes. Her sister loves spin class, so there must be something great about it. Never mind that Sara hates group exercise and that the SoulCycle studio is forty minutes across town. Or maybe it's Megan who needs to make more money as a single mom, so she decides to take on a side hustle in direct sales. She's not really into the product and is mortified at the idea selling in front of a crowd, but her best friend has been really successful at it and she's sure she can be too. Or maybe you're an entrepreneur who dropped out of college because you struggled to learn in a classroom environment. You learned every single thing you know about business on the job through your own research, but when you need that learning the most, you decide that the best thing to do is pursue the one type of learning you absolutely hate.

Friends, personal growth is supposed to be personal.

It's not one size fits all. It has to be customized to you and the way you learn best, or it's never going to stick. Be strict about your goal but flexible in how you get there. Sara should have committed to putting on her favorite music and training for a race. She loves hip-hop and being outside, so she could have customized her workouts to her personality and achieved real results. Megan should have gotten a job at her favorite local coffee shop. She can pick up extra hours while the kids are with their dad, and she gets to chat with the people who come in and be in an environment that she loves.

And me? It took me a minute (and several thousand dollars in nonrefundable tuition), but I eventually recognized that I needed to learn this skill for my business the same way I'd learned every other skill. I asked myself, *Are there books I could read? Conferences I could attend? Could I hire someone? Could I be more honest about what I did and didn't understand in order to get clarity?*

The answer to all of these was, of course!

Was it easy to learn about a topic I'm not particularly interested in without a clear outline about what to do next? No. Was it comfortable to admit to people that I couldn't understand the financials I'd pretended to comprehend before? Absolutely not. But what was the alternative?

My grandpa's voice in my head rang out—louder than my negative self-talk.

I had always figured it out before. I will always figure it out. So I got to work. I learned the difference between a balance sheet and a P&L in a YouTube video. I went to business conference after business conference and sat down front for every session on accounting—even though it seemed duller to me than watching paint dry. At one such business conference I happened to take a class by Keith J. Cunningham. (I'm listing him by name in case any of you happen to struggle with this same insecurity. Find a way to see him speak live!) I have never had someone explain business finances to me as clearly or as simply as he did that day. I literally cried like a baby because I finally understood things I hadn't before. I mean, who in the world sobs over basic accounting principles?

Someone who thought she wasn't smart enough to ever comprehend them.

That's the craziest part about not feeling like we're enough to achieve our dreams. The only way to prove that you are is to get yourself to the other side of doubt. That's much harder to do if you're following someone else's path. You need to focus on what has worked for you in the past and apply those ideas to this new venture. You also need to believe in your possibility instead of focusing on the probability.

Not having the knowledge just makes you teachable, not stupid. Not being in shape just makes you moldable, not lazy. Not having the experience just makes you eager, not ignorant. Flip the script and force yourself to see the positive where you've only seen negative. What are the advantages of not knowing, not understanding, not conquering, not having, not achieving your goals yet? The *yet* matters. The yet reminds us that we have a whole week, month, life ahead of us to become who we were made to be.

You are enough. Today. As you are. Stop beating yourself up for being on the beginning side of *yet*, no matter what age you are. *Yet* is your potential. *Yet* is a promise. *Yet* is what keeps you moving forward. *Yet* is a gift, and you are enough to get to the other side of it.

For me, getting past this limiting belief in myself as an entrepreneur came with acknowledging all the things I *had done* instead of focusing on the things I hadn't. There's a great exercise for this I learned years ago that I think might be helpful for you if you're doubting whether you can do something. Write a letter to yourself, from yourself. More specifically, write from your tenacity, from the part of you that never gave up, from the exact opposite place of your fear. Write from your self-assurance. Write from your heart and your gut and the piece of you who always gets what she sets her mind to.

When I ask women to do this at our conference, there's always this moment of confusion. "But I haven't done anything," they tell me. "I don't have anything to write down."

Sis, the problem isn't that you aren't accomplished; the problem is that you don't give yourself any credit for the things you have done. You need to write a letter from your truth to extinguish the lies about who you really are. So if you worry that you're overweight and out of shape, then write a letter to yourself about all the times in your life when your body was incredible. Did you play sports as a child? Did you carry a baby inside yourself? Did you grow another human life? Those arms that are too squishy and untoned? How many times have those arms offered love and comfort to other people? How often have those arms helped you care for your family or do your job or create your art? You think your dream is too big, too impossible? Write down all the times you did things nobody thought you could.

I'm going to share with you the very first letter I wrote to myself, and I'll tell you right now that the original letter included a lot of cussing because A) I honestly never planned on anyone reading it, B) sometimes a well-placed f-bomb can fire me up, and C) I love Jesus, but I cuss a little. For today's purposes I've toned it way down and removed the words that might have this book banned in several countries. The original letter still sits inside the spiral-bound notebook I wrote it in that day. I don't have a date on it, but I know I wrote it in the middle of my struggles with my worst insecurities about whether I was smart enough to grow my business. I wrote to me from my persistence.

Dear Rachel,

I am your persistence, and this is what I want you to know about me. I am a badass. I was born in pain and fear, and I fought my way out. I graduated early. I moved to a new city. I got a job I was too young to have, and then another, and then another. I built a company that shouldn't have worked and then another after that. I wrote five books. I'll write even more. I took on foster care and raising five kids. I do stuff that nobody else can do in less time than anyone can believe. I am self-aware. I work hard on myself. I face the hard stuff again and again and again. I don't give up, not ever. Your fear may be powerful, but there is no defining force greater in your life than me, your persistence. You have thirty-three years to serve as an example of that!

This exercise was so powerful for me at the time because I truly didn't give myself credit for all the things I had done. I needed to remind myself of the truth. I may not have had a formal education, but I did all those things I listed, and I continue to do those things. That is what I want you to do today. That is what I want you to do this weekend, and in three months I want you to do it again. Then three months after that, I want you to do it again. Every time that fear of *not enough* shows up for you in whatever stupid way it tends to, I want you to remind yourself of the truth. Not the opinion.

For most of us, women especially, we hold on to some little nugget, some little lie, some limiting belief that we've had since childhood. We've believed it for so long, we don't even question it anymore. We heard something when we were younger and our feelings were tender. Someone said something, someone spoke into your insecurity about yourself, so you've spent a lifetime questioning yourself and accepting what they said as truth. The crazy thing is, it's not true. It's an opinion.

1+1=2 is fact.

Gravity exists here on earth. Fact.

Water can extinguish fire. Fact.

You being "enough" of anything? Opinion. Someone else's opinion, or maybe your own, but either way, it is not grounded in any actual reality other than the weight you give it. So how much of your life are you living—or rather, not living—because you've been treating an opinion as a truth?

Here's what's so crazy about the idea of enough. Whatever your issues with not believing you are enough, that is the opinion someone else gave you, whether intentional or not, and you have accepted it and made it a doctrine in your life.

We never boil it down like that. We never really think, *Oh, I don't feel like I'm enough, because the media told me so, because my aunt said something to me once, because a girl in eighth grade commented on this and that became my reality.* Have you ever thought about how ludicrous it is to be living your life, to be making choices to hold yourself back from your goals, to not try things, to not put yourself out there because of something some random person said to you once upon a time? Whether it came from a voice of authority or a chick on the internet, if you're hesitating because of someone else telling you that you are not enough, you're still living your life and making choices for yourself, and, subsequently, your family, based on someone else's opinion.

Other people don't get to tell you what you can have!

Someone else doesn't get to tell you who you can be!

The world doesn't get to decide what you get to try.

You are the only one who can make that decision.

Here's the flip side of that. You've got to stop blaming your problems on the world. You can't be like, "Well, I got teased my entire adolescence, so now I'm insecure." Or, "My parents did these things to me, so now I can't cope."

I'm not belittling the trauma we hold from our childhoods. It's so incredibly harmful to walk through trauma, particularly at a time in life when we're so malleable to other people's opinions. But here's the deal. High school's over. Junior high was a long time ago. You are not a little girl anymore, and you cannot keep living your life with a seventh grader's mentality, no matter how painful seventh grade was. You have to decide right now that you're going to take hold of your life, and you are going to let all of that other crap fall away because it doesn't matter. Because whoever said the thing to you, your mom or your sister or the mean girl or the mean boy in high school or whoever it was, they don't get an opinion on your life. They're not in the ring. They're not in the game. They're not the one taking the punches. That's you.

It's a simultaneous thing. You can't live your life for their opinions, and you also can't keep blaming them. You need to embrace your path. You need to accept that whatever happened did happen and choose to be mindful of the steps that you've got to take now to heal and get past those things. You cannot keep living in the excuses of something that happened fifteen or twenty years ago. Because, seriously, how is that working for you?

I know there are people right now who are thinking, *But you don't know what they did. You don't know what I went through.* You're right, I don't. But I do know that if your past is still affecting your life today in a negative way, holding on to it is not helping you.

Does it make you feel better about yourself? Does it make you kinder to people when you live in that state of misery, in the state of, "I'm too fat. I'm too thin. I'm too young. I'm too old. I'm too . . ."? How is it making you feel?

It's making you feel like crap. Nobody is living in a place of not enough and happy about it. Nobody is inspired and making great choices and enthusiastic and excited for every day while they are living in a state of not enough.

The amazing thing is that this is all perception. It's all what you believe to be true. And you get to decide what you believe. If we were girlfriends in real life I would shake your shoulders and remind you that you get to decide.

I am living proof that your past does not determine your future.

I am a living, breathing example.

I am your friend, Rachel, and I am telling you that I walked through trauma and I walked through pain and I have been bullied and I have felt ugly and unworthy and not enough in a hundred different ways. And I have decided to reclaim my life. I have reclaimed it and fought back against the lies and the limiting beliefs over and over and over again. I have built on that strength by looking at what is true, not what is opinion. And you can too.

I CAN'T PURSUE MY DREAM AND STILL BE A GOOD MOM/ DAUGHTER/EMPLOYEE

You can remove the word *mom* from this excuse and replace it with anything of your choosing: wife, sister, Christian, friend, fill-in-the-blank.

I hate this excuse.

Like, it actually pisses me off. Not because you might believe it, but because I did too. Do you know how many years I wasted trying to live my life to please everyone else? Do you know how long I beat myself up because I liked to work when all the other moms I knew wanted to stay at home? Most of us will grapple with this, and the vast majority of those who do won't pursue anything that might come at the expense of anyone else's happiness.

You want to join a gym, but that would require your husband to watch the baby so you can go work out and he doesn't like to watch the baby? Oh, shoot, well, I guess you can't go. Or, you want to move to a new city, but your family is super close and your mom will freak out if you're not nearby? Okay, I guess you'll just live forever right where you are. Or, you want to use your retirement traveling the world like you always dreamed of, but your daughter was counting on having you nearby to help her with the kids? All right, you better let that vision for your life go.

After all, their happiness matters more than yours does, right? They matter more than you do. The only way to be a good mother, daughter, sister, friend, or whatever is to show up for the other parties exactly how they want you to, when they want you to, right?

Ladies, you get one chance at this—literally only one chance at this life—and you have no idea when your chance might be over. You cannot waste it living only for everyone else.

I don't mean that you should be wholly selfish. I don't mean that you should assume life is only about you and what makes you happy. Part of being in a family or a relationship or a community means showing up for others. The problem is that most women I know don't struggle to show up for others; they struggle to show up for themselves.

I was talking with my dad the other day about the idea for this book. I told him that I wanted to write about pursuing and achieving goals. I told him how many women send me notes asking me how to find the courage to do that. He told me to tell you to be selfish.

"You know what they told me on the first day of class for my PhD?"

My dad always, always starts any story with a question, knowing full well his audience doesn't know the answer. I used to hate it as a child because I assumed he just liked to prove his superior intellect. As an adult, though, I can look back and see that he was teaching us, from a very early age, to work through a problem before waiting for someone to tell us the answer. Now, of course, I do the exact same thing to my kids and cringe to imagine what my eight-year-old self would think of it. In any event, I didn't have an answer for him that day.

"No, Daddy, what did they tell you?"

"They told us to be selfish. They told us that getting a PhD later in life was something you did for yourself and nobody else. They told us that it wouldn't be long before our spouse or our kids or our boss got frustrated by our classes or our homework or how long it takes to write a thesis. They told us if we weren't selfish with this one thing—our dream of having a doctorate—we'd let someone else talk us out of it."

I'm going to assume that you spend a good deal of your life thinking about others and caring about others and being a great family member and employee and friend. But I'm going to tell you, at least as far as your goal is concerned, that you're allowed to focus on it even if it means that you'll miss some time with the people you care about. I'm also going to encourage you to ask yourself (just like in the previous chapter) if something is true or if something is an opinion.

There are two extremely well-known opinions that play deeply into the narrative about what you can and can't be simultaneously. The first is work-life balance. The idea that work and life can ever be perfectly in balance is an opinion.

It's the million-dollar question for every working mom, right, ladies? How do you balance your job and your family? It's a valid question and worth discussing if for no other reason than that it's reassuring to hear other working moms struggle with this too. My thoughts on this topic are really quite strong, and I don't mind telling you exactly what I've said on numerous business panels over the last decade.

Work-life balance is a myth.

More than that, it's a hurtful myth, because I don't think anyone actually achieves it and yet we feel positive that other women somehow have. Someone somewhere mentioned it as a possibility—their opinion, mind you—and the media seemed to latch on. So when we feel off balance and are struggling to keep all our balls in the air, we assume it's just because we haven't figured out work-life balance. It becomes one more thing we're failing at as moms, beyond forgetting it was "weird and wacky hair day" at school and buying the wrong kind of yogurt. Ugh! I detest anything that makes women feel wrong or less than, so allow me to debunk this ridiculous idea.

Work-life balance. Its description implies that those two things live in harmony, perfectly divided up on the scale of your life. My work and home life have never, ever been balanced evenly on any level. Even when I was a seventeen-year-old sandwich maker at the Sub Station in my hometown. Even then there were days when a big project at school meant that I couldn't work as many hours. Or accepting a lucrative Saturday shift (ripe with tip money) meant that I couldn't hang out with my friends. Work and personal life will always battle each other for supremacy because both require your full attention to be successful. It's not bad or wrong; it's just how life works.

Sometimes my boys have school activities or doctor's appointments and I have to leave work to be present for those. Likewise, right now as I sit holed up at the only desk in our house (in my big boys' room), my entire family is having a grand time downstairs by the pool. I can hear them down there laughing and singing along to pop music. They're drinking LaCroix and living their best lives, and I'm up here . . . writing this book. Pursuing my dream of being an author who encourages other women means that sometimes I will have to miss out on pool time in order to make it happen. The scale is never balanced; it constantly shifts back and forth based on what needs my attention right this second. I think that's real for most of us no matter what stage of life we're in, and the only way we're going to get past this mythology that some people have it all figured out is to start being honest about what our lives and priorities really look like. Here, I'll go first . . .

MYSELF

In my early days as a mom and entrepreneur I wasn't a priority at all. I would run myself ragged, taking care of everyone else and never once worrying about how it all might affect me. This was a disaster. I got really sick at least once a year. I was always stressed out. I was always struggling with my weight. It was a mess. Then someone pointed out that I couldn't take care of anyone properly if I didn't first take care of myself. My health and well-being are now my biggest priority. I get eight hours of sleep every night. Yes, eight. Not six or even seven. Eight full hours. I eat well, I drink water by the bucket load, I haven't let Diet Coke touch my lips in over four years. Yes, I'm still addicted to coffee, but we can't win 'em all! I took up running and get in at least twelve miles a week. I carve out several hours a week for prayer, church, and volunteer work because my faith is extremely important to me. I don't think the goal is ever to be balanced, ladies. I think the goal is to be centered. Centered means that you feel grounded and at peace with yourself. Centered means that you can't be knocked off balance regardless of how chaotic things become. If I prioritize myself and make sure I'm centered, then everything else runs smoothly . . . even when it's running at a hundred miles an hour!

MY MARRIAGE

I'm sure many parents would naturally list their children as their first priority, but my marriage will always be the most important relationship in my life. Dave and I have a weekly date night, and we take an extravagant annual vacation together—wait for it—*without our children*. When we're at home we're playing interference with three little boys and our queen bee, Noah Elizabeth, so it's essential that we also get to hang out with each other regularly and act like real-live adults. Because we're both so supportive of each other's careers, it can be really easy to start neglecting our relationship, which has happened numerous times over the years. So rather than risk our marriage slipping into an unhealthy place, we've agreed to make each other a priority. We don't want to have a good marriage or even a great one. We want to have an exceptional marriage, and exceptional requires intentionality.

MY KIDS

I have four children: Jackson, Sawyer, Ford, and Noah. So even when I'm not at work, I'm always on the go. There's morning routine and school drop-off and dinner, baths, books, and bedtime. Then the weekends when we run from sports events to birthday parties and back again. That is a picture of what life looks like today with the kids, but let me back up and tell you about the first two years of running my company. I worked like a maniac. I was often in the office by eight in the morning, which means I was never able to do school drop-off. I got snarky notes from moms at school about missing field trips and bake sales, and I cried myself to sleep about them more nights than I can count. Nobody ever sent snarky notes to my husband for having to work during a field trip—but that's a diatribe for another time. Most evenings I got home around seven, which means I missed dinner. It was a really chaotic season, but that kind of workload is also part of being an entrepreneur and running a start-up. Some people will argue that I lost valuable time with my kids, and I won't disagree. But those three little boys also watched their mom build a company from the ground up. They watched me grow that company to something so big that their daddy came to work there too. They've seen first-hand the power of hard work and dedication, and I'm proud of the example I've set for them. That, for me, in that season, was another way of prioritizing my kids, just with a longer-term vision in mind.

MY WORK

I won't pretend that there weren't times when work didn't take up most of my attention. I also won't pretend that those weren't the times that were hardest on my marriage, my health, and my ability to be the kind of mom I want to be. Now that I'm more established in my career, I'm better able to get my work done during office hours. Also, being five years into this business means I have the help of an incredible staff so it doesn't all fall on my shoulders. My work is a priority for sure, but that looks different in my current season than it had to look in past ones.

———

Remember, figuring out how to juggle all the parts of your life in a healthy way is a scale that slides back and forth. Some seasons of your life will require more attention in one area than another, and that's okay. Someone once said it was possible to be in balance, but that's only their opinion. You get to decide whether or not it's true.

The other opinion that affects our narratives about what we can and can't be at the same time dives into an area of life that I know won't apply to every woman reading this, but it will apply to a vast majority—and the ones who suffer from it are drowning in it. I want to talk about it. I want us all to be aware that it's happening so we can, as a community, take power away from this insidious thing.

Mommy guilt.

You guys, mommy guilt is bullshit!

There, I said it. I don't know if my editor will even let me keep that in here, but if we're going to hold on to one cussword in this book, Jessica, let it be that line right there!

Mommy guilt, in case you haven't ever experienced it personally, is this gross, horrendous, cancerous thing that lodges itself in your heart and creeps its way to your head where it festers forever—unless you actively choose to kill it. Mommy guilt likes to remind you on the regular of all the ways you're failing your children. Some women struggle with guilt on topics like going to work. Others struggle under the weight of guilt associated with everything from wanting time for themselves to not feeding their kids the right kind of blueberries. And I guess, if that was the only thing you had to worry about, maybe it wouldn't be so bad, but being a mom means there are 967 things to worry about on any given day. So not only are you responsible for someone else's clothes and shelter and dental hygiene, but you're also going to go ahead and beat yourself up for those 967 choices you're making *as you're making them* and think that this will empower you to be better next time? No way. This is only going to confuse and overwhelm you and zap you of whatever confidence you had in yourself as a mom, which, let's be honest, is tenuous on the best of days.

I can already hear the critiques on this one. *Well, you told us to be self-aware. You told us we should be honest about the areas where we can improve.* You're right. The problem is that mommy guilt isn't about self-awareness. Mommy guilt is about self-destruction. Part of growth in any area of life is a willingness to make changes to improve. But mommy guilt isn't really about improving, and, more often than not, it's debilitating. And yet we go back to it again and again.

Hear me when I say this: It doesn't serve you in any way. It doesn't serve your children either.

I said something like this recently on a live stream, and a commenter said something like, "No, guilt is so important. Feeling guilty is how we know we're doing something wrong. Guilt is God's way of telling us we're making bad choices."

Holy crap.

No, seriously. That's a load of crap wrapped up and pretending to be holy.

I don't care what religion you were raised in. You weren't taught guilt and shame by your creator. You were taught guilt and shame by people. That means whatever your people thought was shameful is what you learned to be ashamed of. Whatever your family or the influential people in your life thought was something to feel guilty about is what you have guilt about now.

Allow me to give you a way-too-personal example of this. I grew up in the eighties as a Pentecostal preacher's daughter. Suffice it to say, I was not taught to view my sexuality as something good. In fact, I wasn't taught to view my sexuality at all for any reason at any time. That's something I was supposed to "save for marriage." Nobody told me exactly what I was saving or what

I should do with it once I did get married. It's not any great surprise or any great originality to say that I was super uncomfortable getting comfortable with sex. My entire life nobody ever spoke to me about sex, except as this thing that was shameful to give away before a certain time. The problem is that even after that time came I couldn't let go of the shame I'd learned to associate with it. It took me years of work to get past this, and I'm happy to report that now my sex life with my husband is fantastic, thank-you-very-much. But the shame I felt having sex with my husband in the beginning was very real, and I don't believe for one second that this guilt I was feeling was God telling me sex with my husband was wrong. Guilt and shame are not from God, so please don't allow yourself to assume that your mommy guilt is something divine.

Mommy guilt only works to make you question everything you have done, are doing, or might consider doing in the future. Everywhere you look, articles and books and shows suggest this or recommend that. The moms at school only like this brand or that style, and heaven forbid you parent differently than your sister-in-law or how your husband was raised.

Stop the madness!

Number one, dang it, you are doing your freaking best! The fact that you're experiencing any guilt right now tells me that you care about your children and you're trying. You're not always going to be the exact kind of mom you wish you were, even when you're trying your hardest. Today I was trying to put sunscreen on Noah's chubby cheeks, and she fell backward and bonked the back of her head on the wood floor. Then she cried like the world was ending. You guys, I was trying to put SPF 80+ sunscreen on her to keep her safe, and I accidentally made her trip over her swim diaper. I was trying my best, and I still somehow managed to suck at it! That is life! That is parenting! When did we pass some law that we're supposed to do this flawlessly?

When I was little we rolled around—without seat belts—in the back of a station wagon. Nobody cared about car seats or automobile safety. One of my friends' moms laughs and laughs if you try to talk to her about safe pregnancy practices. "Darling," she'll say as she waves her hand in your general direction. "It was the sixties. I had a martini every single day during all three of my pregnancies." I mean, what kind of screwed-up *Mad Men* situation was going on back then?

We're all just doing our best, sis, and beating yourself up when you're trying so hard isn't going to help you do it better next time. You'll be a better mama next month than you were this month, and five years from now you'll be better still. Two decades from now you'll horrify some new mother when you tell her the barbaric things you did when your kids were still small. In the meantime, hopefully you'll work to improve in all areas of your life—including parenting—but I promise you it doesn't serve you in any way to castigate yourself now.

It's possible to pursue something for yourself while simultaneously showing up well for the people you love. It's possible to be a great mother and a great entrepreneur. It's possible to be an awesome wife and still want to get together regularly with your girlfriends. It's possible to be this and that. It's possible to decide that you're going to be centered in who you are and what matters most to you and let other people's opinions fall away. Don't buy into the hype or the pressure or the guilt that you've got to be one or the other. Maybe that's true for other people, maybe that's their opinion, but only you get to decide what's true for you.

EXCUSE 6:

I'M TERRIFIED OF FAILURE

Eight hundred and fifty thousand people watched me fail.

Let's go ahead and start right there, because I know for many of you the idea of falling short in front of even a small group of witnesses is terrifying. Eight. Hundred. Fifty. Thousand. They watched me set a goal, publicly talk about how much I wanted it, and then they saw the aftermath when it didn't happen.

It went down like this.

Like most red-blooded American authors, I have long dreamed of writing a *New York Times* bestseller. For those of you who aren't familiar with this mythical distinction, making it onto this list is basically the unicorn of the publishing world. I think at one time it was all dependent on book sales, but somewhere along the way it became more nebulous. It seems nobody—save the people who work there—can tell you exactly how you get on it. It has to do with sales and press and buzz and, I assume, some form of ritual sacrifice.

My last book, *Girl, Wash Your Face*, was my sixth one to go out into the world, and I knew it would have the best chance of making it onto the list. It's worth saying real quick that I fully understand that a random list doesn't determine my book's, or my own, worth. In fact, to some people it might be a ridiculous target to aim for. After all, it's about the work, it's about the women who loved it, it's about the gift of having your writing in book form in the first place. But we all have dreams we hold close to our hearts. We all have hopes that really only make sense to us. Becoming a *New York Times* bestselling author was mine. It had been my birthday-candle wish for the last fifteen years. It's what ran through my head when I wished upon a star or blew dandelion seeds into the wind. If forced to give you a rationale behind it, I suppose it's because it would feel validating. My entrance into the publishing world wasn't exactly smooth, and even though my fan base has grown with every subsequent release, I guess there's a part of me that would love acknowledgment. Like, *Hey, the publishing community is sorry about the complex it gave you when it told you no one would ever buy your book. JK. You're actually a decent writer!*

So, anyway, I'd dreamed about it for years but never admitted it to anyone because I didn't want anyone to know, lest they judge me for not making it. But this time around, I decided to bring everyone in on the dream. I decided to tell my online audience (at the time, 850,000 women all over the world) about this longtime hope of mine. I figured if it did happen, then they would share in the victory. After all, they're the ones who support me. And if it didn't happen, well, it would certainly be a lesson for us all.

The thing is, as a public figure you're never supposed to call your shot. If you just keep your hopes and dreams locked up inside your mind or within a small trusted circle, then no one will be let down by your failures, because they didn't know what the goal was in the first place. This tactic also means that the public can be surprised and delighted by any success you have. They never know what you're working on, so any achievement feels like a happy little coincidence, fate smiling down on you again.

The issue for me with this way of thinking is that it feels disingenuous. It feels like faking. Here I am telling you to be courageous and brave and to do big things and dare to reach for something mighty. Here I am telling you that failure doesn't matter and other people's opinions are none of your business, but then simultaneously I'm just going to keep all of my big hopes close to the vest? That feels hypocritical.

I strive to tell you guys about everything I'm going through (or have gone through), because I don't think it serves any of us to pretend. So, with *Girl, Wash Your Face* I did the thing an author is never supposed to do. I called my shot. Four months before the release of the book I told everyone (and by "everyone," I mean you guys who follow me on social media) that I have always dreamed of being a *New York Times* bestselling author. This was my sixth book and I'd had years of dreaming about this, and so I talked about it—a lot. It became a rallying cry for women all over the world. Not only was it my dream, but many of you got fired up on my behalf. You dreamed my dream right along with me.

Then came the fateful day. It was Valentine's Day, exactly a week after the book came out, and unfortunately for him, it was also my husband's birthday. That afternoon I found out my wish hadn't come true. *Girl, Wash Your Face* didn't make the *New York Times* bestseller list.

I felt so sad, and honestly I felt embarrassed. I felt like I'd asked my tribe to buy into something that then I couldn't deliver. It was crushing. I cried like a baby, and I spent a few days in the dumps. But I came to a conclusion pretty quickly. Even with all the sadness and embarrassment, I wouldn't take my goal back. I go on social media every single day and tell other women to follow their dreams. I wake up and do live streams and tell you that your goals are important and worth chasing. I write over and over again that failure is a part of life. Failure means that you're living. Failure means you're trying. So what kind of friend would I be if I didn't practice that in my own life?

I had called my shot, voiced my big, crazy, audacious dream. I had told 850,000 people I was aiming for something, and they had all watched me fail. But here's the truth. If you aim at what you can hit, you'll likely get there every time: never any higher, never any bigger, never any better. But if you aim far above your own head, even when you fail you'll fly so much higher than you can imagine.

I would rather fly. I would rather dream. I would rather fall on my face over and over again. I will continue to tell you what I'm aiming at, because I hope that if you watch me fall publicly and stand back up again and again and keep going, then you'll think, *What if . . .* for yourself.

What if you sign up for a marathon?
What if you go back to school?
What if you start that bakery?
What if you quit your job?
What if you take up hip-hop dancing?
What if you go into ministry?
What if you write a book?
What if you start a podcast?

You have dreams. I know you do, and I also know that many of you hold back because you're afraid that others will see you stumble. Let them watch! Let them see what grit looks like! Let them see the mistakes! Let them watch the missteps! Let them see you dust yourself off again and again and again and keep going.

Do you know how many times I have failed as I've built my business and pursued my dreams over the last fourteen years? I'm sure most of you won't remember, but I will never forget each and every lesson I learned along the way.

What does it take to get back up when you've been knocked down? As an entrepreneur I've been knocked down (or tripped up by my own fumbling) again and again. When I was younger I imagined that at some point I'd gain enough experience to avoid failure altogether. Bless my tiny, business-baby heart! This level of success only makes my failures much more public and much larger in scale.

Remember that time I launched The Chic Site in Italy?

Remember that time an employee stole money from me and I had no idea?

Remember when I decided to be a florist as well as a wedding planner?

Remember when I added on luxury gift baskets too?

Nobody wanted the flowers or the gift baskets, in case you're wondering.

My list of failures is miles long. I'm totally aware of how much time and money they cost me along the way. But here's the deal: every single one of those mistakes has taught me something to ensure they don't happen again. Knowing something great can be mined from the ashes means I don't beat myself up when I don't get it right. It means I stand back up quicker, more determined than ever. A mistake that you learn from is how you build best practices. It's only truly a failure when you're so afraid to look at it that you can't move forward. If you can't move forward you will never, ever make it across the finish line.

Ten weeks after the book came out, the impossible happened— or maybe not impossible, but unbelievable to me. *Girl, Wash Your*

Face became a *New York Times* bestseller. I can tell you that when the publisher called to let me know, I literally fell to my knees. I was so stunned. I called Dave at work. I made his assistant pull him out of a meeting.

"I made the list," I whispered when he called me back.

His screams and cheers broke whatever dam I had up when I found out. I cried like a baby. That night we went home and had a drink we'd been planning for a decade. Ten years earlier someone had given us a very expensive bottle of Dom Pérignon. The bottle was so fancy I felt like we should reserve it for something special. At the time, I thought of the biggest, loftiest dream I could imagine and labeled that bottle with my goal: *"New York Times* Bestseller" scrawled across a piece of tape and stuck to the neck.

For ten years it sat in our fridge. It moved from our first town-house to the little fixer-upper to the home I wrote all of my books in. The bottle was covered in dust and had been shoved to the back of cabinets, spending half a decade in the crisper of our beer fridge. And here's the crazy thing: I labeled that bottle back before I'd ever written a single page of a book. I labeled that bottle half a decade before my first book was published. I had dreamed of being a best-seller since I was eleven years old. I had imagined what it would be like to celebrate by opening that bottle for a decade. That night, after ten years of waiting, we drank that champagne, and it was so much sweeter because of all the years from there to here. It was so much better because I had "failed" again and again on the quest for this goal, and if I hadn't been willing to put myself out there, if I hadn't been willing to let the public see me fail in a hundred differ-ent ways over the years leading up to this moment, I never would have achieved any of it.

I'm so grateful I was a failure. I'm so grateful it's taken me fourteen years of mistakes to get to this place in my career. I'm so grateful that each book I've written has done a little bit better than the last, but not one of them has been an overnight success. My writing career—much like my entrepreneurial career—is a snowball rolling downhill. It's only recently that the mass has picked up enough speed to make the ground shake.

I'm grateful for the small spaces I've inhabited; they taught me how to grow.

I'm grateful for every misstep along the way; they taught me how to run.

I'm grateful for every moment of insecurity; they propelled me to gain a lifetime of confidence earned through practice and study.

Had any of it happened quickly or easily, I might have associated the wins with luck or innate skill. Battling through hardship to get here means I have absolute certainty in this truth: I can achieve anything if I'm willing to work for it. Not because I'm especially gifted, but because I'm especially dedicated to improving along the way.

Sis, don't be afraid of failure. Be afraid of never achieving anything at all because you were too afraid of what others might think of you for trying.

IT'S BEEN DONE BEFORE

It's one of those things we all do, right? We look at her life or her work or her Instagram, and we let her success talk us out of chasing anything for ourselves. We stop ourselves from writing that book, opening that business, building that app, starting that nonprofit, because someone else has already done it.

It's been done before.

Well, of course it has. But, sister, everything has been done before. Kissing, dating, getting married, winged eyeliner, white jeans, bangs . . . honestly, everything that sounds interesting or cool or like something you might want to try? It's already been done! So why is it that we don't let that detour us in any other scenario except pursuing something big?

Because we need an excuse.

Please note, I didn't call this section of the book "Legitimate Obstacles to Get Around." I called it "Excuses to Let Go Of." The fact that someone has already done the thing you're dreaming of shouldn't be a deterrent; it should be a sign that you're on to something.

Dang, look at Suzy already making rainbow doilies on Etsy— just proves that it's fulfilling and fun to make and sell crafts online.

What's that? Your cousin Emily is already killing it in that direct-sales jewelry company? Oh, I guess that means it really is an incredible place to build community and a side income!

But instead of seeing other people's success or creativity as a good thing, as a sign that pursuing something more for your life has value, you decide that it's a competition and you'd rather not try at all in case you're not as good as she is. Sure, this is partly about feeling like you're not enough, but it's also about the unhealthy game of comparison.

One of the messages I get all the time from women is, "I loved your book and I'd love to be an author, but I could never write like you do." Or, "I've always wanted to do public speaking, but I'm not as good as you are."

Girls, stop comparing your beginning with my middle! Or anyone else's for that matter. What you are reading right now is my eighth book, and I'm not saying it's Pulitzer material, but it's light-years away from my first in terms of skill. Have you ever looked at my Instagram feed and thought it was pretty? Scroll back a couple of years—just for funsies—and see what it looked like when I was just figuring out my personal style or how to not look like a robot in photos. Go look at the blog too; some of those original posts are doozies. You think I'm a good public speaker? Please go peep on my old YouTube videos where I'm speaking at MOPS groups and at the local senior citizen home (I kid you not!). I intentionally keep the older content in my feeds and on my website because, if you ever fall down an internet rabbit hole some night and find some of my original work, I want you to see the progress. I *did not* wake up like this. And that person you're comparing yourself to? Neither did they. You stop yourself from trying because you think it's already been done. Well, of course it has. But it hasn't been done by you.

There's a great Chinese proverb that says, "The best time to plant a tree was twenty years ago. The second-best time is now."

You can keep talking yourself out of the thing you're hoping for, or you can decide that your dream is more powerful than your excuse.

This isn't a question of whether you can do something well, because nearly anything can be learned; this is a question of whether you're humble enough to suck for as long as it takes you to become better. The ability to write well or speak well or do photography or dance or any old thing at all—those are learned and improved over time. But you're never going to get to the place where you become good or better or best if you won't even put your shoes on the starting blocks. We don't know whether you can speak like me or write like Brené Brown or take pictures like Jenna Kutcher. Sister, we can't determine when you'll cross the finish line, because you won't even let yourself show up for the race!

You are talking yourself out of something you haven't even attempted, because you think you can't measure up to how someone else has done it. But this particular excuse is not about your skill. This excuse is about your fear. There are all sorts of different ways this type of fear manifests, so please feel free to identify with the one that describes you best and allow me to drop some truth bombs up in here.

You're afraid that you'll suck because . . . you've never done it before. Let me relieve you of this fear right now. You are going to suck. All beginners do. Because if you were secretly a prodigy at pursuing the dreams of your heart, some long-suffering yet dedicated teacher would have seen it in you long ago. We all saw *Dangerous Minds*. If Michelle Pfeiffer didn't see potential in you by now, you're not going to be perfect right out of the gate. Huzzah! There's zero pressure to be perfect now, so you can just have fun and get better. Your potential for improvement is exponential.

You're afraid that you'll suck because . . . you fail at

everything, so why should this be any different? God's almighty nightgown! Is this really how you speak to yourself? Like, really? Number one, knock it off! You are beautiful and worthy of good things, and if you don't believe that, nobody will. Number two, go get my last book and read about the lies that are hurting you. This kind of belief is crushing and untrue. You have to begin with the way you speak to yourself and the things you believe you deserve before you attempt a new goal. First learn to love yourself well and give yourself credit; then reach for more.

You're afraid that you suck . . . and at least if you never try, no one—especially you—will be able to confirm that. Spoiler alert: this kind of thought doesn't come from an under- achiever who's not good at anything. This kind of thought comes from a perfectionist. And, truthfully, it's lame. There is so much incredible potential inside of you, but you're going to squander it because trying may or may not confirm that you're not as good as you thought you were. Stop being so hard on yourself! It's like that time on *Saved by the Bell* when Jessie succumbed to the pressures of schoolwork and being in her band, Hot Sundae. Spano was a per- fectionist, but rather than admit that it was too much to keep up with it all or concede failure, she got addicted to drugs and had that now-infamous breakdown to a Pointer Sisters song. Don't be Jessie Spano. If you try for your goal, you probably will suck for a minute (see the paragraph about sucking as a beginner), but you won't stay there for long. You'll work to get better, and you won't even need caffeine pills to do it.

Look, here's the irony about this particular excuse: even if you push yourself to confront it, you will keep encountering it for the rest of your life. When we're early on the path to personal growth or on the way to achieving a goal, we often have unrealis- tic expectations of what will happen once we "get there." Like, if you just have the courage to do this one thing, then it will make you invincible to insecurity and indecision for the rest of your life. The reality is that every new mountain you attempt to scale will likely have been traversed by someone before you.

Every. New. Mountain.

That means that once you get over this big goal in front of you—once you get to the summit (I'm really going all in on this analogy, guys)—you'll see another mountain range in the distance. In fact, you'll realize that your mountain was actually just the foothill of something bigger and better. Personal goals are infinite . . . and addictive. Once you achieve one it makes you start to wonder what else you might be capable of.

The answer? Anything you set your mind to.

But first you've got to get over this battle with comparison. Because, friend, if you can't get over your fear of not doing it as well as they do, you'll never have the opportunity to be a trailblazer for someone else.

———

As I work through edits on this book, I'm in the process of creating something that many, many people have done before me. I also have exactly zero qualifications to take on something this massive. About a month from now a documentary we made about my women's conference will be in movie theaters throughout North America. I mean, who in the actual heck do I think I am? Well, I'll tell you who I am not. I'm not a filmmaker or a movie industry insider, and when we started on this project I had no idea how we would pull it off. It's the biggest thing we've ever attempted to do, and it will live in a space—in theater events and later streaming services—that are insanely oversaturated. Not only that, but there are people who are experts in this field and sometimes even they fail at it, so what in the world makes me think we have a shot? Well, frankly, the project being successful wasn't what made me want to do it. In fact, I believe if I had focused on whether or not it would make money, I would have started to obsess over all the ways I was ill-qualified to take it on. Actually, what motivated me to try and work on something so outside my wheelhouse was, well, you.

As we were planning our conference last year, I received thousands of emails and direct messages from women saying how badly they wanted to attend Rise and how much it would mean for their hearts to have an opportunity to be in our audience. The problem wasn't their desire to attend; the problem was their finances. It's expensive to attend a conference because of travel and hotels and the price of tickets required to cover the cost of renting out a space so large. Many women didn't have it in their budgets, and I took that to heart. For nearly a decade I've been creating content and giving it away for free, and the idea that you might not be able to access something I believe in so passionately really hurt my heart. I spent months trying to figure out a way to bring the conference and the power of reaching for personal growth to women at a price they could afford. Then one day on a random conference call I heard about event cinema, which is a fancy term for putting a live event (like the ballet or a Justin Bieber concert) into movie theaters on a limited run. *Dang it*, I thought. *If the Biebs can do this, I'm pretty sure I can do this!* I asked myself a *what if* question.

What if we made a movie about Rise weekend?

What if I could find someone to partner with us to help get it into theaters?

What if I could give the tribe the chance to create a girls' night out in their own community?

I hope you can understand how insane this idea was. We didn't know how to make a movie or how to get it in theaters or the literally hundreds of steps between there and here. We were the worst kind of dumb—we didn't know what we didn't know. But I didn't spend any time worrying about our lack of knowledge, and honestly, it didn't occur to me to care about who had done it better or how it might be received. I wasn't focused outside myself; I was focused on my *why*. My why was powerful; my why made me feel passionate enough to figure out my *how*.

If you find yourself worried about the idea that someone else has already done it, you need to flip the script on whether that's a bad thing. If someone else has done it, you can research and model behavior and test out your own theories using their road map as some kind of guidance. You can combine their *how* with your *why* to create something epic.

EXCUSE 8:

WHAT WILL THEY THINK?

I started boxing.

And just so we're all clear on this, I don't mean boxing at the 24 Hour Fitness. There's nothing wrong with boxing at your local gym. I just want to make clear the distinction between performing boxing-style moves for cardio at your usual workout spot and going to a real-life boxing gym that's dirty and smelly and blasts Metallica like it's required for the sport. I've only been to a few sessions so far, so for all I know it is required for the sport. My point is, I'm getting real training from someone whose job it is to teach actual fighters how to throw a punch.

The gym I'm going to for this training isn't pretty by any stretch of the imagination. The workout is grueling, and I often feel like I'm going to die or puke up my breakfast smoothie all over the ring. I don't fit in. Imagine a dirty room full of Minotaurs and then me, all five feet, two inches of me with my long, long extensions and my overly dramatic fake lashes. There I am, a thirty-five-year-old mother of four, trying my darndest to slide away from punches lest my trainer knock me upside my head. I'm not exceptionally good at it, though truth be told I've never seen any kind of boxing match, so I'm not totally sure what the end goal is supposed to be. So why do I do it? Why do I keep showing up to try something amongst people who are so much further along than I am? Why do I hang out in a room I don't fit in and keep attempting to learn something I'm not particularly skilled at, all while others watch and judge and draw their own conclusions?

Because it makes me happy.

I like throwing punches and working out to Jay-Z and flipping my hat around backward like a proper tomboy. I love boxing, and I love pushing myself to try something new. Here's the kicker: I don't care what anyone else thinks about that.

But maybe you read that and think, *Okay, big deal! You're comfortable at your boxing gym. I don't know how that's supposed to help me find the courage to start a business as a wedding photographer!* Well, how about this? There are two types of people in the world. Nonjudgmental people, who aren't ever going to think badly of you for anything you do regardless of the outcome, and judgmental people, who are jerks. These jerks are probably working through their own issues and we'll pray for them, but, at the end of the day, judgmental people are going to judge you *no matter what!* If they're going to judge you either way, then you may as well go for it. You may as well live your life. You may as well be true to who you are and what you value and let go of how it will be received.

On Mondays my kids have karate. On other days there is baseball practice and piano practice and then karate practice again. We might have an audition for the school musical. We might have a dine-out night to support the PTA. We might have playdates or dentist appointments or simply need to make the trip (for the millionth time) to get everyone's hair cut. There are so many things to keep up with when you have four kids, and I don't always remember them, no matter how hard I try.

Yesterday the school called to tell me that Ford is the very last child (out of all the incoming kindergartners) who still needs to turn in his paperwork.

You guys, I didn't even know what paperwork she was talking about!

Which brings me back to karate practice. Karate practice takes two hours (not including drive time), while first my youngest and then my big boys try to work their way up to the next belt color. Those two hours happen during a weekday afternoon when I should technically be working. But I want the boys to have the opportunity to do something cool, to not be held back by my schedule, which is something that happens more often than not. So, if I can make it work, I get off early and take them to practice. Then I sit down on the blue carpet amongst water bottles and flip-flops, and at some point, I open up my laptop and start working through emails, or book edits that are due on Friday, or the timeline for one of our live events.

And inevitably I start to get looks from the other parents.

Now maybe I'm being presumptuous. Maybe those looks are actually because they like my computer case, or they think my hair looks especially good in that topknot today. But if I had to guess, I'd say their looks are more about the fact that I'm working when I should be wholly devoted to watching my kids master their front kick. Some insecure part of me—the one that used to worry quite a bit about what other mothers thought about my parenting style—considers putting the computer away. But then this is the trade-off, or maybe *perk* is a better word.

So many working moms wish they could make it to practice, even if it meant they were building a spreadsheet on Excel while their children karate-chopped the air to the Pokémon soundtrack. What a gift that I get to have that experience! So I don't put the laptop away. I remind myself that this is part of the deal, that these boys of mine will always know what hard work and dedication look like. I remind myself that someday when they're grown men it will never occur to them that a woman can't start and build and run a successful company, because that was always part of their reality.

God willing, I'm the only mom my kids will ever know, and I honestly don't know any other way to make this all work—for all of us—without multitasking sometimes. So I refuse to teach them that you should pursue your dreams but simultaneously be ashamed of them. If I don't want that for them as adults, I need to model that behavior for them now. I can't worry about what the other moms at practice think of me, and you can't worry about what the other moms, or your in-laws, or the PTA think of you. All you can do as a working mom is try your best. All you can do as a recent college grad is try your best. All you can do as a fifty-something divorcée is try your best. All you can do at any stage and season of life is try your best, and someone else's opinion of how you're doing or what you're doing is . . . none of your business.

You know this, friends. I know you do! So why is it that your dreams are still hiding out in your heart instead of taking shape in your hands? It's not a fear of failure that keeps you in this place; it's a fear of what other people will think of your failure.

OPO, other people's opinions. You down with it? Because if you are, you're giving all your power away.

The opinion of the other moms at school? The opinion of the Hulks in my boxing gym? The opinion of strangers on the internet or my parents or even my fans? The second I start to give inordinate weight to any of it is the second my priorities get out of alignment. When other people's expectations start to dictate your actions, you're lost. Your hope, your dreams, your sense of self . . . it all gets lost.

You want to make real strides for yourself and your goals this year? Stop caring about what "they" think of you. Stop giving power to someone else's opinions.

Inevitably, when I say something like this the question that comes back is about accountability and whether we can truly maintain our integrity if we have no sounding board. First of all, you know what's right and wrong. You know what's true. Down in your gut, you know how the best version of yourself would live out this day, this life you've been given. You may not always get to that place, but you know what it is you're striving for. So don't underestimate that.

Secondly, if you're truly blessed, you will have people in your life who are confidants and true friends. Their wisdom will be your counsel, and you can seek them out when you need to. But— and here's the place where people get tripped up—there is a big difference between wanting someone's opinion and needing their approval. The latter typically comes disguised as the former. We ask for an opinion because we're feeling unsure about something, and often if we can find someone to agree we somehow justify the idea as good or bad.

Yesterday I made this mistake with my husband. He is my best friend and counselor, and I still had to separate his opinion from what I really wanted. I have this idea for a new book. A new fiction book. I haven't written fiction since I wrapped up my Girls series, but (as often happens when you're in the middle of writing a book) I started daydreaming about my next book. This happens partly because you're deep in a creative headspace and mostly because writing books (no matter how many you do) is super hard. Fantasizing about being finished and working on the next thing is the carrot you dangle to get you through big writing days. So this new novel, it's my carrot, and I got excited enough to tell Dave about it. And in doing so, I opened myself up for opinions.

His opinion was that the plot sounded a lot like something else and that it also sounded a little convoluted. He said it in the nicest way, truly just a harmless thought as part of our little brainstorming session. The problem is not that he offered his opinion; the problem is that I immediately started to adjust my thoughts about the book. I immediately started to wonder if maybe he was right and my idea was wrong and I should just scrap it. But the truth is . . . it doesn't matter.

It doesn't matter if Dave is right. It doesn't matter if the experts are right. It doesn't matter what anyone else thinks or believes. The idea, the dream, the goal is my own. The second I start looking for other people to validate it, I begin to lose steam and momentum. When you're in the early stages of an idea or a goal, you're the most insecure, which means you're easily swayed by what other people might think or believe. You're most easily talked out of an idea you might have loved or into an idea you might regret when you allow other people's opinions to color your plans.

It's like when you ask someone to review or critique the first draft of your manuscript when you're only halfway done. When I ask someone to read an unfinished draft, it's because I'm looking for validation. It's usually because I'm struggling and thinking I'm a terrible writer, and I want someone whose opinion I admire to tell me to keep going. The truth is, no one else can validate you enough to finish a first draft. No one can validate you enough to follow through on the dream you've laid out for yourself. Even the most encouraging coach on the planet can't make you finish the race. You're going to have to find it in yourself to chase it down all on your own.

But what's the harm, right? If you still finish it yourself in the end, why does it matter whether you look for someone else to validate your idea in the beginning? Because, while other people can't help you finish, they can certainly—even if unintentionally—talk you out of trying.

I wish I could just snap my fingers and make it so that you no longer felt trapped under the weight of other people's opinions and expectations, but I know it's not that easy. It's a hard habit to break, but make no mistake, it's a habit and a choice. We can choose to not allow that weight in our lives, but since we're all probably operating under some negative opinions, we also need to learn how to get out from under what is already there. And that starts with understanding exactly what kind of opinions we're dealing with.

Here's the deal. There are two kinds of negative opinions: substantiated and hearsay. Substantiated means that you know for sure the negative opinion is there. Someone tells you the things they don't like about you—straight up to your face, like a Drake song. Maybe they're family, maybe they're friends, maybe they're random strangers on the internet. These kinds of substantiated opinions are delivered two possible ways. Just follow me down this flow chart. I promise we're going somewhere.

The first possible presentation of a negative opinion is thoughtful and kind. It's given to you by someone who cares about you, and they're concerned about a choice that you're making. But even when their heart is in the right place, there's a lot of nuance here. Is this really about you? Or is their concern grounded in their perception that what you're doing is wrong? Remember our conversation about other people's perceptions of what's shameful? Please see my OPO Flow Chart for how to proceed here.

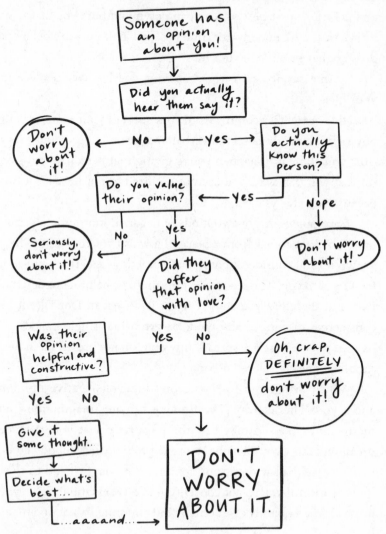

The other way you might possibly hear someone's negative opinion about you is in a hurtful way. This is when whoever is offering the opinion—family member, friend, stranger—doesn't come with the intent to offer constructive feedback or to help you get better or to show you true concern. Their intent is to tease you and belittle you at best or tear you down and hurt you at worst. Either way, ain't nobody got time for that! This person's behavior does not have a place in your life.

Let me say it again: this behavior doesn't have a place in your life.

I don't care if it's coming from your sister or your mom or your boyfriend. Nobody deserves verbal and mental abuse, and every time you allow it to happen you're giving that person permission to treat you that way. You are not required to put up with it just because you always have.

To recap, we've got two kinds of negative substantiated opinions. The first comes from a place of love, so you're going to be a grown-up and consider it but not accept it as gospel truth unless it feels right to you. The second isn't meant to be helpful but destructive, and therefore you should reject it. Reject it! Don't let it be considered, discussed, absorbed, or given one single particle of oxygen to help that fire spread. Any opinion not presented in love should not be considered. Period.

Which brings me to the second kind of negative opinion about you. The hearsay. The figment of your imagination—no matter how likely it may be—the negativity that you've made up all on your own. Eleanor Roosevelt told us that nobody could make us feel bad without our consent. I'm going to add to that. Be very careful you're not consenting to let your mind make you feel bad when nobody else actually did anything. What do I mean by that?

Perhaps you're *pretty sure* your mother-in-law disapproves of you. Or you're *almost positive* that your cousin Crystal's snarky comment on Facebook was aimed in your direction. Maybe you know for a fact that the girls you went to high school with who you now know only through social media *would* make fun of you if they saw you trying to do something new. In all of these instances, none of these negative opinions are actually substantiated, and therefore, you're really just sabotaging yourself.

Nobody has said anything. Nobody has done anything. Maybe your new mother-in-law does disapprove of you, and maybe she just misses her son and feels anxious about how she'll fit into your life. Maybe your cousin Crystal was aiming that comment in your direction, but you and I both know that Crystal is the *worst!* She used to give you titty twisters—this is the person whose opinion you're going to worry about?

The irony is, most of the time, nobody is actually thinking about you. Nobody actually cares what you're up to, and if they do they're not judging you or making fun of you behind your back. It's not like you hang out with a bunch of ogres, right?

And if they do dislike you, it doesn't matter. It. Doesn't. Matter. But more than that, assuming that someone thinks the worst of you when you have no real evidence to back that up isn't about them—it's about you. You're letting their opinion control your life, and you don't even know if they really have one! It's all in your own thoughts. You're just wrapping it up and blaming it on other people so you don't have to take responsibility.

The truth is, it doesn't matter what they think of you; it matters what *you* think of you. Hard as it is to reconcile, someone else's opinion only holds power if you allow it to. If you actively take steps and intentionally begin to live without obsessing over what other people think, it will be the most freeing decision of your life.

EXCUSE 9:

GOOD GIRLS DON'T HUSTLE

I'm a hustler, baby.
—JAY-Z

Don't you hate it when an author starts a chapter with a quote? As a longtime book nerd, I have read approximately seventy thousand novels, and the quote thing has always felt a little self-aggrandizing to me. Like, "Oh, just read this elegant prose from Tennyson, and prepare yourself for a similar level of talent!" It's even more annoying when the quote in question has literally nothing to do with the chapter you're reading.

No. Thing.

And you find yourself wondering, *Is this esoteric? Am I supposed to understand the correlation between a Whitman quote and this dragon-shapeshifter love story?* You would be shocked to know how many books about vampires falling in love with single moms or aliens falling in love with librarians start each chapter with a random quote.

Yes, I read horrendously cheesy romance novels. Stop judging me.

The point is, I hate chapters starting with quotes.

But this chapter was a bonus in the last book—shout-out to all of you who snagged the Hustler's Edition!—and I loved it so much and felt like it was such an important topic that it gave me the idea to write *this book*, so we're going to start with the most iconic line on hustling I can think of. A Jay-Z lyric.

A bonus chapter is like Equestria or a Kardashian birthday party—*anything* can happen here. So I'm bringing in Jay-Z lyrics just for my gals who are chasing down a dream, who want something more and aren't afraid of hard work and audacious goals!

Let's talk about hustle.

I have been an overachiever for as long as I can remember. I was a dreamer from the very beginning. I would imagine elaborate scenarios my future grown-up self would be part of. I knew what my mansion would look like, could foresee the vacations I'd take, the prince I'd marry, and the horses I'd own. Horses because, well, I was seven and having my own horse was the ultimate fantasy. I was going to name her Calliope, and I'd only ride her wearing the special tan pants that rich, equestrian-inclined girls wore in Lifetime movies circa 1991.

A little girl daydreaming isn't anything unique, but perhaps what *was* unique was I knew even then that I could achieve anything—if I was willing to work for it.

I don't remember anyone ever saying that to me. Maybe I just understood it through observation and osmosis. When you grow up in a home that struggles financially, it doesn't bother you until you're exposed to the opposite. I realized at a very young age that there were people who didn't live paycheck to paycheck, who didn't scream at each other over money, who could walk into Target and buy anything they wanted.

I was eleven when my goals for my future solidified. My

parents had broken up again—it happened so many times over the course of my life, I honestly cannot tell you what number it was that time. The difference in this particular instance was that my mom decided to move out, and she insisted I come with her. Nobody asked me what I wanted or gave me a say in the matter. They simply announced that it was happening. My three older siblings would stay with my dad in our family home, and I would move into a crappy apartment with my mom. It was one of the darker years of my childhood.

I rarely had access to my siblings, and the financial strain of parents who were now dividing resources to pay for two places to live meant that we had even less than before. I have a photo from that time of my eleventh birthday party with a handful of friends from school in this run-down, shabby apartment. I remember being embarrassed. I remember the boxed cake mix baked in an old Pyrex. I remember that we couldn't afford decorations. I remember being hyperaware of two things. First, I didn't want the kind of life where I lacked funds for special occasions. Second, it's not very convincing to assert your independence—from my mother, in this case—if you don't have the financial means to back it up.

I vowed to myself *that day* that I would be wealthy when I grew up. It was my birthday-candle wish. I stood in that tiny dining room on stained carpet, in front of the yard-sale table, and I promised myself something better. *I will never live like this when I have the ability to prevent it.* I was vehement in this: someday I would be rich.

I'm not supposed to say that, I know. Social media is filled with hundreds of male CEOs and self-made entrepreneurs who tout the power of wealth and the justification for achieving it. But, if you're a woman, it's frowned upon. It's impolite. It's not something *good girls* do.

Good girls don't talk about money, and they certainly don't claim it as a life goal, regardless of their reasons why.

What I learned in childhood? "You get what you get, and you don't throw a fit."

That meant I should be happy with whatever life handed me, gracious and thankful for whatever came my way. But what was coming my way as a child and later as a teenager was a mostly crappy existence, and because I was a child, I couldn't do anything to change it. But I knew after that birthday party that the second I was in control I would never be forced to settle again.

There is a *big* difference between gratitude for your life and blind acceptance of whatever comes your way.

I wanted more.

I wanted more than I had grown up with. I wanted more access. I wanted more experiences. I wanted more knowledge. I wanted more challenges. I wanted more influence. I wanted the ability to help others who were in difficult financial places, because I knew exactly how they felt—I understood even then that monetary resources would make that possible. I wanted so many big, grandiose things. When I was a child, people thought it was adorable. They'd pat me on the head and tell me how precious it was, but in my early twenties I quickly learned what was and wasn't acceptable to my family, friends, or husband.

When I started my own company, everyone saluted my moxie, but two years later, when I was pregnant with my first child, people immediately asked when I would be quitting. The business, they concluded, was just this cute thing I was doing to keep myself busy until my real calling started: being a stay-at-home mom (SAHM).

It's worth stopping right here to qualify that statement. I sincerely believe there is no harder job and no more important job than being a SAHM. I have so much stinking respect for my SAHM friends, and I'm not for one second implying otherwise when I tell you that it's just not for me. Next to my husband, my children are my greatest blessings. But, y'all, if I had to stay at home with them full-time, I'm not entirely sure any of us would survive. It's not my spiritual gifting. It's not in my wheelhouse.

You know what *is* in my wheelhouse? Building a successful business, managing a team, writing books, giving keynote speeches, crushing it on social media, strategizing, branding, PR, and planning live events where a thousand women fly in from all over the world to be inspired. But at the time, none of those things were proven. I was still so new to business. I only had an idea in my heart and a fire in my belly. I was figuring out how to run a business using books at the library and Google. I asked a hundred thousand questions to anyone who could offer wisdom.

It was slow going at first, but, dude, I was *going*. I got my first client, and I worked my butt off. I treated that one single client like they were the last opportunity I'd ever get. I didn't have money, I didn't have a ton of experience, but I *did have* an unmatchable work ethic, and I let it shine. I got the next client based on a referral from that first one. I did events for basically nothing in order to build up my portfolio. I took on any client I could find.

I was essentially like, Do you have a pulse *and* a need to plan a party? You do? *I'm in!*

So when I got pregnant and had to explain my choices over and over again to well-intentioned family members, it honestly sucked. For the first time in my whole life I understood that *other people* didn't agree with the life I'd imagined for myself. They didn't like the idea of a working mom, even though they'd accepted it early on when we needed the money. A couple of years later, when Dave's salary increased enough that it was clear I didn't "have to work," the passive-aggressive people around me began to vocalize displeasure outright. Even when you're strong, even when you're committed to your goal, it's hard not to second-guess yourself or take on guilt when it's coming at you from every angle.

Open disapproval wasn't enough to make me change my course, but I did stop claiming my course as my own. I wouldn't recognize it until years later, but those opinions began to wear me down. I was like a piece of glass that gets thrown into the ocean. Other people's opinions became my waves, their judgment the sand I was tossed against over and over until it began to chip away at all my jagged edges. I know that as a society we tend to think that being smooth and pretty, everything worn to a soft, rounded edge, is what we should aspire to. But the more I grow and learn and think about it, the more I understand that your jagged edges—the parts of you that stick out in odd directions and don't match everyone else—those are what make you uniquely you.

My unique qualities? I am a leader. I am a teacher. I've built two successful companies through hard work and hustle and the wealth of knowledge that can be found from a Google search bar. My goal is simple, even if it's grandiose: I want women to understand that they have the power to change their lives. It's at the core of everything I do. It's the platform I've built everything else on, and I truly believe it's what I was put on this earth to do. I'm building a media empire around the idea.

No, I did not mistype. Yes, I just said A. Media. *Empire.*

Not a company, not a side hustle, not a small business—an empire.

The world tells me that good girls don't hustle, and they certainly don't stick a flag in the ground and audaciously shout that they want to be a media mogul. They for sure don't feel so passionately about it that they have the word *mogul* tattooed on their wrist.

I know I'm not the only one who has ever bumped up against

the expectations of others and then backed down because of them. In a desire to find community, I constantly seek out other women in leadership, and what I find again and again are women doing just what I did. They're downplaying all that they've achieved, because they've been taught that it makes others feel uncomfortable.

You guys, *astounding* women are doing this. Women who have built hundred-million-dollar companies or are running massive teams with unbelievable revenues. Those kinds of women are afraid to admit that they're good at their jobs or that they love what they do. Interacting with them has made me feel less alone, has made me understand that this is something many other women face down. So I'm telling you my story in the hopes that if you're like us, you know there's a tribe of ladies who feel the same way, even if not everyone has found the courage to say it out loud yet.

It's okay to want something more for your life. In fact, hang out with me long enough, and you'll discover that it's one of the things I value most in people. Drive, hustle, the desire to work as hard as you can to chase down a goal? That's my jam. Hustle is my love language.

I love a hustler. I love someone who is unabashed about what they want for their lives and *refuses* to let anyone talk them out of it. I don't mean that they never feel intimidated by their own audacity. I don't mean that they don't occasionally fall into the trap of other people's opinions. The hustlers I know, they're human and they face the same insecurities as the rest of us. But when push comes to shove, they don't overthink it or debate it; they just put their heads down and get back to work. That's what *hustle* means to me: it means that you're willing to work for it, *whatever it is*, whatever you want, and you don't assume anyone is going to give it to you, but you know it can be yours.

Society tends to raise boys to go after what they want and

tends to raise girls to go after the boys. I'm here to tell you that it doesn't matter what society thinks about you or your dreams. Heck, it doesn't matter what your family, your closest friends, or your spouse think about your dreams either. All that *really* matters is how badly you want those dreams and what you're willing to do to make them happen.

Laurel Thatcher Ulrich said, "Well-behaved women seldom make history," and there are hundreds of years of evidence to back her up.[1]

Sojourner Truth, Susan B. Anthony, the suffragettes, Marie Curie, Malala Yousafzai, Oprah, Beyoncé—not one of these women put up with the expectations placed on them by the society or the time period they were born into. None of them downplayed their gifts, resources, or the access they were given. Those women, and so many others like them, lived into their God-given strengths and talents regardless of what the world thought of them, sometimes against almost impossible odds and life-threatening oppression.

Are you a hustler? Me too. Do you secretly want to be, but you're afraid of what other people might think or say? I've been there.

For many women the weight of other people's opinions will be too big a burden to carry; they won't be able to step outside the safety net because they're too scared. But that's not us. We're willing to go after it, we're willing to be audacious, and we're willing to take it on because the chance to live into our full potential is worth any backlash that comes our way.

Some say good girls don't hustle. Well, I'm okay with that. I care more about changing the world than I do about its opinion of me.

PART II

BEHAVIORS TO ADOPT

be·hav·ior[1]

bəˈhāvyər/

noun

1. the way in which one acts or conducts oneself, especially toward others.

"good behavior"

2. the way in which an animal or person acts in response to a particular situation or stimulus.

synonyms: conduct, deportment, bearing, actions, doings

Your behaviors are the way you act day in and day out. Your behaviors are your habits. They manifest in the actions you take, the words you say, and the way you live your life. What is most important to understand about your behaviors is that they are a choice. They don't feel like a choice because the vast majority of your behaviors are made without conscious thought. They're habits that have ingrained themselves in your life, but they are choices we make, whether consciously or unconsciously. Which means every single day you choose to be this person . . . whether you realize it or not. You choose to believe what you believe and accept what you accept, and these behaviors can either help you immensely or harm you without you ever really knowing it. Now that we've let go of the many excuses that hinder us from pursuing our dreams, we need to take some steps toward them. This section is a list of the behaviors I adopted that helped me get to my goals, and I hope they'll help you do the same.

BEHAVIOR 1:

STOP ASKING PERMISSION

Okay, sisters, I know not everyone is comfortable with the word *feminist*. As I mentioned earlier, *feminist* simply means you believe men and women should have equal rights, but I understand there's a world of other meanings wrapped up in the word for many women, and I'm not trying to convince you otherwise. I only bring it up now because this chapter is going to feel like the most feministy feminist words you've ever heard from me, and if that's not your cup of tea, your inclination is going to be to skip this chapter.

Don't skip this chapter.

You absolutely don't have to burn your bra in the streets, but you are a grown woman and owe it to yourself to consider this idea. This chapter is not about men versus women and how we should navigate the disparity. This chapter is about the truth that most cultures have been set up—since the beginning of time—as patriarchal. This means that in most societies men have more power (or all the power) and therefore more control.

It doesn't matter whether you believe this is good or bad, natural or misguided—girl, you do *you!*—but for the purpose of this book and chasing down your goals, it matters that you at least consider how this kind of structure might affect your belief in yourself. After all, if you were raised to believe that men know best, that men are the authority, how much faith does that teach you to have in yourself and your opinions as a woman?

I was on a business trip recently and stopped by a bookstore in the airport to grab something for the plane. I ended up picking up this incredible book called *Women & Power: A Manifesto*. It's a really interesting study of the history of women speaking publicly. Not women speaking, but women being allowed to (or rather not allowed to) speak in public forums. You should absolutely check it out. It's a rich history and well written, and you can read it in two hours. Personally, I've never really studied—and so therefore never focused on—how little access women were once given to use their voices or offer their opinions. Oh sure, I've read all about the suffragettes and how hard women fought for the right to vote, but I never stopped to consider the long history of pain and torture and even death that happened in the hundreds of years leading up to that time.

There is this incredible part in the book that I thought was so powerful. It was the idea that for most of us, the voice of authority in our lives growing up was male. And if we grew up and started working or grew up and married a man, then it's possible that the voice of authority stayed male. The person in charge, the person who told you what to do, who told you what was right and wrong, often, was a man.

If that man was good and wise and had your best interests at heart, then that might have instilled the belief in you that he knew best. That's powerful enough on its own, but what if that man in your life wasn't good? What if he was hurtful or cruel? What if he had his best interests at heart instead of your own? He was still in charge, he still got to make the decisions, and he still got to affect your life.

There's this saying that's been around forever: "If you don't see it, how do you know you can be it?" If your example of "right" was always male, do you think it would occur to you naturally that you as a woman have the authority to be whoever and whatever you want to be? Do you think you'd easily come to believe that you have the right and the power and the might to pursue your own dreams just for yourself? Or, do you think it's possible that you might seek permission or even approval from people other than yourself because that was your normal?

I was raised with a voice of authority that was male. My daddy is a strong and very forceful personality, and he demanded total obedience. I learned to live in hope of his approval and terrified of his displeasure. Then I met my husband when I was nineteen years old, and though he is a very different kind of man, I can recognize in retrospect that I transferred my feelings about my father to my husband. I was utterly codependent. I lived every day to please him and make him happy, and if he was unhappy—even if it wasn't about me—it was crippling. I would drown in anxiety until I could do something or say something to change his mood.

I remember about seven years ago he'd had a bad day at work and he was really frustrated when he got home. I went immediately into "fix it" mode. I was like, "Can I make you a drink? Are you hungry? You want to watch a movie? You want to have sex?" and he looked at me very firmly but very kindly and said, "Rachel, I'm in a bad mood, and I'll get over it. It's okay if I'm upset. You don't have to make it better. It's not your job to make sure I'm happy."

Holy crap, you guys. It was a freaking epiphany! It really never occurred to me that I should just let him process his feelings and it wasn't my job to fix them. I had been raised in a house where we did everything possible to keep Daddy happy, and I didn't know there was any other way to be.

Consequently, when I began to understand that the entire purpose for my life wasn't to please someone else, I began to consider things I hadn't before. Like, what if I could make decisions for myself? What if I stopped making every choice in my life about what would please others most? What if sometimes I just did what I wanted to do? What if I stopped asking permission?

I didn't even realize I was doing it back then, but for the first probably ten years of my marriage I had asked Dave's permission to do everything. Not because he told me to, but because that's what I thought was normal and I brought it into our marriage with me.

"Do you care if I go to the grocery store?"

"Do you mind if I have dinner with Mandy on Thursday night?"

"Hey, is it cool if I eat the last of the Girl Scout cookies?"

I did this years before we had children, so this wasn't even like a "Hey, I want to do this activity, and I'm going to need you to cover childcare" sort of thing. This was me seriously needing his sanction to do anything in my life, because I didn't want my desires to inconvenience him in any way.

I look back on those years, and I thank God that I married a good man. It would have been so easy for him to take advantage of me or abuse the power he had over me if he'd been inclined to.

Friends, if you're reading this, I'm going to assume you're a grown-up woman. Grown-up women don't ask permission. There is absolutely a way to be your own person while also being part of a great relationship with someone else. It is absolutely possible to manage your priorities, your responsibilities, and your personal desires in a way that stays true to you and the people you love.

It happens when you stop asking permission to be yourself.

It happens when you stop caring more about what they think of your dream than what you think of your dream.

It happens when you put more value into your self-care than you put into whether they'll be inconvenienced by it.

You're allowed to want to be your best self, to pursue your dream, even if they don't understand it. You're allowed to push for something more, even if they don't like it. You're allowed to take time away from your kids, even if it's an inconvenience to the person who has to watch them. You're allowed to do something, even if it makes your partner uncomfortable. You're allowed to tell people who you are and what you need instead of first asking if they're all right with it. You're allowed to simply exist without permissions or opinions or qualifiers.

———

I'm trying to recall when I first heard the term *girl boss*.

Certainly it reached the heights of popularity when Sophia Amoruso published her book. At the time, I lined up to buy it like every other self-respecting, self-taught female entrepreneur. Reading her story was inspiring and motivational, and I honestly didn't give much thought to the title because I was so fired up to read what was inside.

But then I started to see the term (and subsequent offshoots) everywhere . . . #GirlBoss #BossBabe #EntrepreneHER. Women of every age and background picked up the moniker and ran with it. It became a popular trend on social media that still hasn't died down years later. It's part of the vernacular now. It's tossed around at conferences and has become a title that young women in entrepreneurial studies programs aspire to.

And it makes my blood boil.

I want to stand on a soapbox and rant about this particular topic and how it plays into the male voice of authority, but instead I'll ask a question. Do you know what it means to qualify something? I ask, because when I was younger, I don't think I would have stopped to consider the pet name of "girl boss" for women like me. I would never have questioned what a hashtag might say about women in business in general. When I bring up the act of qualifying something in panel discussions at one conference after another, only a handful of people respond saying they do know about it. And so I read the definition aloud:

qual·i·fy[1]
> kwŏl'ə-fī'
> verb
> 1. To *modify, limit, or restrict,* as by listing exceptions or reservations
> 2. To make less harsh or severe; moderate

Before coming to run my company, my husband was a high-level executive at one of the largest media companies on the planet. He led a worldwide team of more people than I can keep track of. He worked his way up from an assistant with drive and determination. He's also never—not one single time—had someone give him a label for the work he does based on his gender.

To qualify the term *boss* by adding *girl* or *babe* or *honey* or *pink* or whatever other ridiculous, antiquated gender-role assignment the media thinks is cute this month, is at the least disrespectful and at the worst damaging to the way young women view themselves and to our fight for equality in the business world. And the worst part is, women are the ones who are perpetrating this! Women are the ones who are stamping this label on stationery and T-shirts and pinnable quotes, all under the guise that it's helpful and inspiring to a younger generation.

On some level, they're right: owning or running a company or a team is inspiring to a younger generation. But if our daughters have the courage and grit to pick up that baton, don't belittle their efforts by saying it's pretty good *for a girl*. We don't call them "girl doctors" or "girl lawyers" or "girl nominees for president of the United States of America." Those positions were hard-fought to achieve, and they demand respect. So does this.

Being a boss has been one of the greatest privileges and challenges of my life. Being a boss takes guts and tenacity. Being a boss takes hustle and strength. Getting to the level of boss takes hard work—oftentimes harder than it takes for our male counterparts because, in many industries, we're fighting our way into a boys' club. You might call that kind of person a rebel, a rogue, a leader, but there's nothing gender specific about it.

I bring it up now because I want to remind you that you do not need anyone's permission to be yourself, and you also don't need to conform and twist and rebrand your goal to make it more palatable for them. You don't need to present yourself in a certain light to be loved and accepted. The people who deserve to be in your life will care about who you—the real you—actually are, even if it takes some getting used to. Even if you're different from every other woman they know. Even if you're different from the woman they fell in love with.

Be the kind of woman you want to be.

Be the kind of woman who is proud to be herself.

Be the kind of woman who has so much love inside her that she won't be tempted to change herself in order to get love from others.

Be the kind of woman who focuses more on being interested than on other people thinking she's interesting.

Be the kind of woman who laughs loudly and often.

Be the kind of woman who is generous—no matter how much money is in your bank account, you have a wealth of resources to offer others.

Be the kind of woman who spends a lifetime learning, because knowledge is power and those who think they know it all are often the dumbest among us.

Be the kind of woman both your eleven-year-old self and your ninety-year-old self would be proud of.

Be the kind of woman who shows up for her life.

Be the kind of woman who understands that she was made for more.

Be the kind of woman who believes that she is capable of doing amazing things in this world.

Be the kind of woman whose own dreams make her nervous—and then go ahead and do them anyway.

Be the kind of woman who never asks permission to be herself.

BEHAVIOR 2:

CHOOSE ONE DREAM AND GO ALL IN

Here's the thing I believe about a goal that often annoys people: you can only focus on one at a time.

You. Can. Only. Focus. On. One. At. A. Time.

If I were allowed to put emojis into a nonfiction book, you better believe there'd be a little aggressive handclap in between each one of those words.

This one is aimed at all my dreamers who are like, "I want to author a book, but I'm also a singer-songwriter and I'm thinking about getting my real-estate license and I also want to work with homeless animals and start a charity to bring endangered species into senior citizens' homes to comfort the aged."

No.

First of all, even if your list isn't quite so elaborate, even if all the things on it support one another, *even then* it's not going to be effective. If it were effective, it would have worked already.

Secondly, that list isn't one filled with dreams. That is a list filled with some cool ideas. You need to understand the difference.

When I say *dream*, I mean something you greatly desire. I mean that you're fantasizing about something and imagining what it would be like regularly. I mean that when you think about it your heart beats faster and your palms get sweaty like an Eminem song.

Mom's spaghetti.

Many people won't get the Eminem joke I just made, but that's okay. Three people did, and as long as someone understands my humor, that's all I care about.

Back to the dream versus great idea thing. When people list off the nineteen things they're "dreaming of," my response is always the same: Which one makes you most excited? If you could choose only one of them to work on for the next decade, which would it be? If only one of them could be successful, which would you choose?

The thing is . . . they always have one. Always.

But they surround their single greatest dream with a bunch of great ideas. They list out all sorts of possibilities, because that way they can say it's all just for fun. That way their options are endless. That way, if chasing the dream becomes too difficult, they can quit and tell themselves it wasn't what they truly wanted anyway.

See, if you only pick one dream there is no plan B. If you want to take the island, burn the boats. If you want to actually achieve your dreams, you can only pursue one at a time. I believe completely in going all in on one single dream, and when you achieve that one, then you can move on to the next. But splitting your attention is splitting your focus and your energy, which means you're not likely to make much progress.

When it comes to personal growth, women often approach it like a buffet. They want to work on a little bit of this and a little bit of that. They reason that all the areas of their lives are important, and so they should try to fix them all at once. Maybe that's possible for some people, but I can tell you what's worked for me, in contrast, is focus.

I have a whole life outside of the pursuit of my dreams. So do you, I assume. I've got a marriage and children and a career and groceries and dishes and a thousand other things. I don't have time to waste time. If I'm going to fight for my right to pursue something new for myself, I need it to be as effective as possible. And to be effective, it's got to be totally focused.

In the past, whenever I set out to start my diet and my exercise program and finally write my novel, my energy and enthusiasm wouldn't survive the week. There were too many priorities, too many things to keep track of. I got overwhelmed easily and couldn't keep up with it all.

When everything is important, nothing is important.

I found success when I learned to focus, and focus requires choosing one thing. It's hard for first-timers to commit to only one area when they're passionate about growth. What they don't realize is that a goal is like a harbor. When the tide rises in the harbor, all the boats rise.

This amazing thing happens when you start to grow in one area of your life: other areas improve with it. If you drop a handful of pebbles into a lake, you'll move the water around a bit. If you drop a boulder into a lake—meaning, if you put all your energy into one area—the impact is incredible. The ripple effects of that choice spread out in all directions.

For clarity's sake, I'd like to mention that it's very possible to grow in multiple areas of your life once you've achieved success in one area and established it as a habit. For instance, I am able to maintain my health and fitness regimen while pursuing a new goal, because health and fitness are habits in my life now. But, if I had tried to conquer them simultaneously or attempted to take them on while starting my company, let's say, I wouldn't have been successful.

The question then becomes, How do you decide? How do you pick the right thing to focus on next? Well, if you're me, you narrow it down using a process I like to call "10, 10, 1."

If you've never heard of 10, 10, 1 before, that's because I made it up . . . but I did trademark it, because it's a good idea and I'm not a dummy. Like most things in life I figure out a process that works for me, and when pressed to explain it, I write it out and give it a snappy title. See: my entire publishing career.

Ten years.

Ten dreams.

One goal.

Who do you want to be in ten years? What are the ten dreams that would make that a reality for you? Which one of those dreams are you going to turn into a goal and focus on next? 10, 10, 1.

Let's look at it a bit more closely together.

TEN YEARS

I like to encourage people to start by closing their eyes and imagining the best version of themselves. Imagine that a decade of time has gone by, and you are living your best possible ideal for yourself and your life. Dream big. Don't put any restriction on it. Don't overthink it; just allow yourself to envision the most magnificent possible future version of yourself. A decade in the future, what is the very best version of yourself doing? What does she look like? How does she go about her day? How does she speak to people she loves? How is she loved in return? What kind of clothes does she wear? What kind of car does she drive? Is she a great cook? Does she love to read? Does she love to run?

Get as specific as you possibly can. Where do you go on vacation?

What's your favorite restaurant to eat at now that your life is different? What kind of food do you consume? What does it feel like to go throughout your day? Are you optimistic? Are you encouraging to others? After a decade of working on yourself and growing as a woman, how much joy is there in your life? Who's in your life? What's your week like? How do you treat people? How do they treat you?

Just let your dreams run absolutely wild. Are you happy? Are you energetic? Are you driven? Do you feel ambitious? What's your relationship like with your family members? Do you own a home, and what does it look like? Do you have kids, do you have a family, are you married? What's the best of the best?

Now go bigger. What's a bigger version of the best version of you? Living every day in the best state that you know how to be. What do you do for work? What is the highest value that your future self holds? Is it family, is it loyalty, is it growth? Be as specific as you can be.

Now, without a second of judgment or overthinking it, I want you to write down everything that you just thought of as fast as you can. I don't want you to forget any of it; I want that future version of you to be seared inside your brain.

The best version of me is . . .

When I'm at my best, I . . .

Don't hold back. This is not the time to think it through or tell yourself to slow down. This is not the time for realistic; this is the time to think as big as you can possibly go.

Hopefully, this exercise helped you paint a clear picture in your mind of a lot of different awesome things your future self can take part in. Personally, I like to do this once or twice a year and create a vision board (like in fifth grade when you glue a bunch of magazine clippings to poster paper) so I've got a visual to go along with my mental imagery.

That is the first step; that's you in ten years.

Now here is how you narrow it down.

TEN DREAMS

Turn your ten years into ten dreams. If those ten dreams came true, they would make your vision a reality. So, if you saw a future that was completely financially free, maybe your dreams would be things like making a six-figure salary, being completely debt-free, etc. But maybe your future dream self is also healthy and happy and energetic. Add becoming a marathon runner and vegetarian to the mix. The important thing is, again, to be specific. The list of dreams is how that future vision manifests for *you*.

Often, when we do this, we come up with more than ten, but it's essential to narrow it down. Focus matters, remember? Choose ten dreams that, if they were to come true, would make your future self real.

Now here's the key: write down those ten dreams in a notebook every single day. And write them as if they've already happened.

I do this every day of my life because I want the repetition to instill in my head and my heart where my focus should be. I want to remind myself *who* I should be. I write them as if they've already happened, because I read somewhere once that your sub-conscious focuses on what you give it. If you tell yourself (and your subconscious), "I'm going to make a million dollars," you don't end up focusing on the goal but on the words *going to*. It becomes like a to-do list for your brain. You didn't give it direction. You didn't ask your mind to help you figure out how. You only told it that you were going to do something, which isn't especially powerful no matter how big a goal you set for yourself, because you create to-do lists all the time. What makes this something your brain should take notice of?

What if instead you told yourself, "I have a million dollars in the bank"? That's specific. That's an outcome. That's a direction to head. *Going to* is something in the future. *Have* is present tense, which means your subconscious starts focusing on how to make that real right now. I don't actually have a million dollars in the bank . . . yet. But I'm working on it.

Some items on my list are things that I want to achieve; other items are things I can accomplish every day.

"I am an exceptional wife."

That one is on my list. I write it down every day as a reminder of who I am and who I want to be. When I imagine my future best self, she's still drunk in love with Dave Hollis. In the future he's still my best friend, and we still can't keep our hands off each other. Only now we look so much fresher because all our kids are older and we don't have to change diapers or wake up with a teething baby.

I'm careful with the words I write down too. I don't use the word *good*. I don't use the word *great*. I use the word *exceptional*. When I write that sentence about being an exceptional wife every day, I have to ask myself what I did today that made me exceptional. It's a simple prompt to move me into action. It reminds me to text my husband and tell him how hot he looked in those pants or how much I love him and appreciate him. That wouldn't happen if I didn't have the prompt reminding me who I want to be.

Another item on my daily list is kind of obnoxious but, hey, it's my dream list, not yours. I write down, "I only fly first class."

If you follow me on social media, you may have some idea of how often I travel for work. It's a lot, you guys. A lot. I don't mind the travel, because 90 percent of the time I'm on the road to give a keynote speech or motivate a bunch of conference attendees with my unique lyrical stylings and the energy of a springer spaniel. Public speaking is one of my favorite parts of my job, but it also requires focus and energy. It's hard to have either when you're shuffling back and forth across the country on planes. And it's hard to keep up with my current workload so that I can make all those speaking engagements when I'm sitting in coach.

Also, my current workload always involves writing. I'm either writing a book or editing a book or working on an article or a post, and because it's me and I don't know the meaning of the word *private*, almost everything I write tends to be sensitive in nature. Do you know how weird it is to write a chapter on your sex life while a rando guy sits next to you sharing the armrest? I do! I've written on planes for years; there's no other way for me to turn these suckers in on time. And I hate not writing simply because I'm worried about what my neighbor thinks of chapter 5. That's where this dream comes into play.

In my mind, first class is good for one single thing: seat size. I don't care about their weird entrées. I don't care about the free wine. I don't even care about the ability to get on the plane before everyone else. All I care about is that, in first class, I can sit criss-cross applesauce with this computer in my lap. It's so comfortable. It's so far away from the next nearest person. It's the best!

I know this because one time, years ago, Dave used his miles to upgrade me on a flight. Once I got a taste of the promised land, I couldn't stop dreaming about it. So I wrote the words, "I only fly first class." Every day. For months and months. Which means that every day my brain accepted that as truth and helped to make that dream a reality for me.

When I first started writing it on my list, we didn't have that kind of money in our travel budget at work, and just because I wanted it to be true didn't make it so. But after writing it down for about six months, I had an epiphany so dumb I wanted to punch myself in the face for not thinking of it earlier. You're going to laugh. Or maybe you already know how I solved the problem, because it was so obvious to you. I started flying first class because I told people it was part of my travel requirements. Meaning, when companies reached out and said, "Hey, Rachel Hollis is the cat's pajamas, and we'd love to have her fire up our sales force. What would it take to get her here?" my assistant would tell them my speaking rate and, right after it, she'd add the line "plus first-class travel and accommodations."

In the beginning, I was so nervous that people would be annoyed and that I'd miss out on big opportunities or be seen as a diva. But nobody batted an eyelash. First of all, when you've worked to get to a certain place in your career, it's not unusual to request perks you wouldn't have been given when you first started out. Secondly, brands could either afford it or they couldn't, but nobody got mad or sent the villagers to my house with pitchforks. Now I get to fly in the big seats, and I arrive at each work event feeling good and productive and ready to go.

In case you're wondering, I still have that line item on my list. I get to fly first class for work, but I'm not at a place with personal finances where we could do that for our family—yet. Every day I'm reminded about where we're headed.

Now that you have your ten dreams identified, I hope you take my advice and write them down every day. It's a great way to remind yourself daily about who you want to be, but in order to get there you've got to tackle that list with action and focus. The next step is narrowing your focus down to one goal. 10, 10, 1. Ten years becomes ten dreams becomes one goal. Your dream is your ideal; it becomes a goal when you actively begin to pursue it.

ONE GOAL

I want you to ask yourself right now, What is one goal—one thing you can do—that will get you closer to the ten-years-from-now version of yourself the fastest? What is the one goal out of the ten you just finished identifying that you can work on this year? Think it over, then write it down.

To achieve a goal, you need to make sure you have clarity on two things:

1. What are the specifics?
2. How will you measure your progress?

"I want to lose weight" is not specific. Do you want to lose two pounds or a hundred pounds? That's specific.

"I want a body-fat percentage of 24 percent."

"I want to save $5,000."

Those are specific goals that you can measure against.

"I want to do better with my finances." That's garbage. You're already setting yourself up for failure, or you're setting up to give yourself credit for work without making measurable progress. Paying cash for your latte instead of using a credit card could be considered "doing better on finances," but where is it getting you? If your goal is something more along the lines of "I want to save $5,000," you wouldn't have a latte at all.

Your goal also needs to be measurable. You have to be able to judge whether you're making progress or getting closer to where you want to be. A lot of people also say that a goal has to have a time limit, but I don't like that for personal goals because I feel like it sets you up for failure. If you tell yourself you've got to be in shape by the end of February and then you get to mid-February and you haven't done it, you beat yourself up. The intention here is that working on your ideal self is a lifelong process to become who you were meant to be. Lifelong processes don't have a time limit. All that matters is that you keep at it. We're not looking for perfection; we're looking for consistency.

Now, it's not enough to know what your goal is going to be. Many of you probably already knew what you wanted to achieve, and if that was all it took you'd have already claimed it as your own. You've also got to know why you want it so badly. You need to define why it must be yours and use it as leverage to motivate yourself when you want to give up. Remember earlier when I talked about how important your *why* is? *Why* will keep you going even if you don't know how you'll get there.

When I was a little girl, my parents fought a lot. These were extreme fights—punching-holes-in-the-walls kind of fights—and I would hide out in my room to get away from them. I would take myself into the only space that was mine alone—my bed—and I would escape by imagining a place where none of this existed. I would imagine a future where nobody screamed at each other. I would also imagine a future where nobody fought over money. As a child, the greatest vision I could imagine for myself was walking into a store and being able to afford anything I saw. I'm not talking about a watch or designer shoes. I mean being able to afford the brand-name cereal or a new pair of jeans for school. That was the best vision I could have for myself then: a home where nobody fought and the ability to afford things at Wal-Mart.

So that was my goal, and the underlying reasoning for it was something I remember thinking at a really early age: *When I'm in charge, I can live whatever life I want.* When you visualize your future, you have to know where it is you're trying to get to, and you have to give yourself some motivation to keep you on course.

Said another way, you have to know your why. Why does it matter to you?

It's not enough just to want to be thinner. It is enough to want to lose weight so that you can be able to keep up with your kids or have energy for your life. That's leverage.

It's not enough to say, "I want to be rich because I think that would be awesome." It is enough to know what it's like to go without as a kid and to promise yourself that you're never going to live this kind of life again once you have the ability to control it. That's leverage.

You have to know where you're going, and you have to know your why. For those of you who start and stop, start and stop, start and stop, if you've gone off your resolution fifty times before, it's because your why wasn't strong enough.

I used to smoke. I hate to even admit that to you, because it's absolutely terrible. Smoking is the worst. It's so disgusting; it's so bad for your body. But I was nineteen when I started. I thought that cool kids smoked, and I wanted to be cool. Then one night at the company holiday party, I was chatting with this really rad girl who worked in the PR department. She was so hip! She was hipster before hipsters existed, and that night at the holiday party she pulled out a pack of American Spirits. If you aren't familiar with American Spirits, they are basically straight tobacco, way stronger than anything I had ever smoked before, only I didn't know that at the time.

I'd been drinking too much that night, and when cool hipster girl offered me a cigarette, I didn't think anything of it and proceeded to spend the rest of the evening smoking one cigarette after another. I went home from that party and threw up again and again. Everything smelled like that cigarette. I barfed until nothing was left inside my body. I woke up the next morning in my bed wearing nothing but red Isotoner socks. Best I can guess, I had gotten myself undressed, down to the way I came into this world, and then put on those socks for—I don't know—comfort? Then I puked for three hours before passing out. The point is, to this day I cannot smell cigarette smoke without wanting to vomit. I never touched another cigarette again. I had had such a bad experience, had gotten to such a bad place, that I went cold turkey and had zero issues giving it up. I will never go back there again. That's leverage.

You have to have the leverage—you have to know your why—or you will never make change. You have to know what to focus on, or you will never make progress.

BEHAVIOR 3:

EMBRACE YOUR AMBITION

Ambition is not a dirty word.

I don't know if it's because I'm in the midst of writing this book and therefore am ever mindful of the conversations playing out in media right now regarding women, but it seems one popular female author and speaker after another is commenting on the type of women we should all aim to be. This morning I saw yet another repost of a quote on the dangers and pitfalls of ambition in women. I was angry to the point of spitting and simultaneously so sad. Angry, because I don't think it's helpful to make sweeping generalizations about all kinds of ambition and all kinds of women. Sad, because this person has a powerful platform and voice for women all over the world, and I believe this message is a disservice that plays deeply into the narrative many of us grew up with.

Can ambition be dangerous? Absolutely! I've spoken at length about my own struggles with becoming a workaholic, so I know how dangerous and unhealthy that can be. But ambition as a whole? To call it out as utterly wrong feels shortsighted and counter to the call to live into who we were all made to be.

It's important to note the comment wasn't directed toward men. It was calling out the dangers of ambition in women. We need to start having a very real conversation about why we accept truths about ourselves as women that we would never consider for men. If it's not true for everyone, then it shouldn't be true for anyone.

I get that many people believe differently. I get that, depending on where or how you were raised, the idea that we shouldn't hold ourselves to a different standard can seem downright heretical. But just consider it for a minute. When a man wants to push himself in his career, his fitness, his faith, his education, or anything else, this is considered an asset. We want those kinds of people leading our businesses, our churches, or our governments. Ambitious people work to learn more, do more, grow more, and typically they create opportunities for the people around them to do the same. But that's not okay for a woman? What if she's not yet married? What if she's a single mom? Is it okay for her to try hard then, at least until she's got a man to take care of her? I hope you read the sarcasm in that last sentence, because the very idea makes my head want to explode!

We need to get past the idea that certain rules only apply to certain people at particular life stages. If it's not true for all of us, it shouldn't be true for any of us.

My sister-in-law Heather has been a teacher for the last eighteen years. She was an all-American softball player before she got her bachelor's degree in elementary education. She went on to get her master's in school counseling, all while being an outstanding leader in education and a champion for the children in her care. That desire to learn more about her work so she can be more effective at it—that's ambition, and it shouldn't be any less admirable in her than it would be in her brothers.

My friend Susan is leading the charge in foster-care reformation. She's changing the way we love on children in care and surround foster parents with the support they need to do this work. Her ambition is off the charts. She has ambition to open branches of her organization in every city in the United States. She has ambition to make sure every child in foster care feels loved and known and seen. She has ambition to make sure not one more child ages out of the system, ever. It's grandiose and audacious. Her brand of ambition will change the world.

Another girlfriend is a stay-at-home mom who struggled for years with her weight and her self-image. Eighteen months ago, she signed up for her first 10K; her ambition was to make it to the finish line. After she conquered that race, she signed up for a half marathon. She pushed herself to find the time to train and the will to learn how to get herself to her goal. She finished the half marathon and will complete her first full later this fall. Her ambition wasn't to be a CEO or make a million dollars; her ambition was to get fit and healthy so she could be a better woman for herself and mama for her kids. Her kind of ambition changed the family dynamic in her home and the way she looks at life.

Ambition is not a bad thing.

In fact, the definition is downright poetic: "a strong desire to do or to achieve something, typically requiring determination and hard work."[1]

If it weren't for my ambition and determination to create content that would encourage other women, you wouldn't be sitting there reading this book. I mean, we're basically halfway through it right now, so if you thought it was stupid or unhelpful or boring, presumably you would have given up by now. Chances are you're still here because you're getting something out of it. But there wouldn't be anything for you to consume if I hadn't been ambitious about writing it in the first place.

So much of the time, though, we can see ambition as a good

thing only until it's our own, right? It's never really other people's ambition that bothers us. It's our own that feels scary.

What would they think of me if they knew this was my dream? We don't care about what they think, remember?

Well, what if I get too ambitious and obsessive? Why don't we worry about things that are actually happening instead of possible somedays?

Okay, but what if I do go crazy and chase my dream to the detriment of my family and my relationships? Crap, sister, me or someone else who loves you will come over and knock some sense into you! Are you really not allowing yourself to pursue something because of a bunch of made-up possibilities?

Scratch that. Of course you are. You're scared, and I understand what it is to be scared of the unknown. But you're not going to achieve anything if you don't get comfortable with the idea of achievement.

Do you have a goal or a dream? Are you trying to chase something down? Then you better get well acquainted with the idea of ambition. You need to adopt a posture of striving to grow in the ways that matter to your goals. Ambition looks like waking up early; it looks like working after the kids are in bed. Ambition looks like adopting a willingness to admit to the things you don't know and asking for help or doing the research or becoming your own best mentor. Ambition looks like you living in a way others won't so you will have a life others can't. Are you ready to own your ambition?

BEHAVIOR 4:

ASK FOR HELP!

It's the eleventh hour, girls. I was supposed to have given my publisher the edits on this book last week. I had to ask for an extension, and that extension says that this sucker is due today if I want to make my publication date. I want to stress how late in the game I am on this creative process, because then you'll understand how insane it is for me to be adding this chapter right now.

Like, I'm starting a chapter brand new when I'm supposed to have this whole thing safely tucked into an email and off to a lovely gal in Tennessee so she can copyedit it.

Instead, I'm going rogue. And I'm doing it because it occurred to me this morning, like a lightbulb going off, that I completely forgot to include an incredibly vital behavior that you absolutely must adopt into your life. For days I've been wandering around thinking, *I know I'm forgetting to tell them something, I just know it!* And then I remembered what it was, and my only excuse for it not occurring to me originally is that it's such an ingrained behavior for me now that I didn't think about it as something extra to add in. But I get your DMs and your emails and your media-based, emoji-filled messages that are full to the brim with overwhelm, and I am reminded that not every woman does this. So here it is: ask for help!

Ask for some dang help!

You cannot read the chapter on ambition and allow it to fire you up if you aren't also going to figure out what resources you need to get you there. Deciding to take adult tap dancing lessons because they light your heart on fire doesn't just require new patent leather metal-bottomed shoes and a selection of Yelp-recommended dance studios. It also requires someone to watch your kids while you go to class. Ask for help.

Attempting to grow to a new level in your multilevel marketing business doesn't just require classes and webinars and a sick social media presence; it also requires someone to help you around the house since you will have less time for that. Ask for help.

I get it, girls, I do. I know that it feels awkward for the vast majority of us to ask for assistance. For one thing, we hate admitting to anyone—especially ourselves—that we need it. For another, we've somehow gotten this twisted idea that copping to the fact that we can't successfully do it all means that we're weak. Ha! Think about how ludicrous that is. The most powerful people in the world have whole teams that they delegate to. They're getting help in every single direction, from cleaning their houses to expanding their businesses overseas. But you—you with your fledgling business, your loads of laundry, and your two kids under four—you're the one who's supposed to navigate this all alone? Dude. No way. You've got a twisted perception of what success in *any* area of life looks like. And it's not even your fault either.

I blame the media.

Or, more specifically, I blame every perfectly styled, ultra-fabulous-looking woman who's ever been on TV or the internet in the last fifty years who didn't tell us how much assistance it takes to keep her at that level. I blame every magazine who showed us thirty-nine ways to brine a turkey for Thanksgiving but didn't mention asking your sister to stay the night with you the day before so someone was there to help with the baby while you cook for the family. I blame every Nancy Meyers movie with those dreamy houses and all-white wardrobes. Oh, sure, she showed us the zany hardship of navigating a relationship, but she never once showed the staff of people required to keep those mansions clean or those organic gardens tended while our heroine was building up her catering empire.

You've likely only ever seen examples both in real life and on-screen of women doing it all. It seems to me that women either try and handle every single thing on their own and don't admit how much they're struggling, or, worse, they have help, all kinds of help, and won't cop to it. Madeleine Albright once said, "There's a special place in hell for women who don't help other women."[1] Well, I say, there's a special place in hell for women who have the luxury of assistance but won't admit to other women that they do.

I was watching a segment on the *Today Show* a couple of years back, and there was a famous celebrity there sharing her new product line. This woman had young children and a husband whose career was as lucrative and as demanding as her own. I really love this person. She's so beautiful, and she seems like such a genuinely good mama and wife. She's made a big name for herself in the life-style space. She has become the woman that many mamas and homemakers want to be. But when they asked her in the course of the questions how she "does it all"—as in, how did you build this multimillion-dollar business and manage to parent well and be a great wifey?—she looked right at the interviewer and said something like, "Oh, I'm just super organized."

My jaw hit the floor, you guys. She went on to breezily explain how any mom can do just what she does if they apply themselves and work hard.

I was so disappointed in her response, I wanted to cry. Sincerely wanted to cry like a baby. Because here's the deal: this woman has a massive platform, ten times bigger than my own, and on that particular morning I can't imagine how many women were watching her, looking up to her, and hoping for some guidance or inspiration. And she evaded. She had the opportunity to tell all of us what it really takes to live life and have a business at this level while raising young children, and she didn't take it.

There is a zero-percent chance—a ZERO-percent chance—that she doesn't have help. Having spent years and years working with celebrities, I'd guess she's got a housekeeper and at least one nanny, if not two. She's got to have an assistant, and because of their level of celebrity, I bet she and her husband even have some of the higher-level domestic staff you might not have even heard of before. Things like "house managers" and "nutritionist chefs" and, you know what, good for them! I do not begrudge them a single second of their help. I just wish they'd talk about it. By not talking about it they run the risk that it won't occur to *you*. If you see their perfectly prepared dinner on Instagram when you know she was at a photoshoot all day (because you watched it in her feed), it might make you feel bad because you struggle to get dinner on the table even when you've been home all day. It might not occur to you that a housekeeper or a chef helped her prepare that dinner, which perpetuates the myth that you could also "do it all and have it all" if only you'd work harder.

This is a lie from the pits of celebrity hell!

Friends, women operating at the levels you'd like to both personally and professionally are asking for help. Maybe that help comes from their partner. Maybe that help comes from their mama or their sister. Maybe that help comes in the form of a local college student who babysits or a local cleaning lady who scrubs their toilets once a month. There are tons of ways to get help, but to start we need to understand that it's required in the first place before we can take the next step. Nobody does this alone. When I put it so plainly, it seems like common sense, doesn't it? But then we come across terms like *self-made* and start to wonder whether that's still what we should be shooting for.

I love the term *self-made*, particularly when it's used in reference to my own success, because only I know how much work it took to get from there to here. I was the one who got up before the sun. I was the one who logged all the miles on business trips. I was the one who cried over the P&L and stressed about making payroll. Me, me, me. For years I held on to that title and the idea of doing it all on my own, because it fired me up and helped me keep going when it felt so lonely on this entrepreneurial journey. In the last few years I've realized something, though. I am self-made . . . and, also, not.

It's only recently that I understood that no one is ever truly self-made, because it's impossible to build big things entirely by yourself. A whole team of people helped me build my company over the last decade. A massive tribe (who started out as a handful of followers) told their friends about my work and are still the greatest hype squad I know. It took family and babysitters and nannies to help keep our family afloat during the times I had to put in extra hours. It took the world's biggest cheerleader as a husband, celebrating my wins and covering my losses both financially and emotionally in those early years.

It took a village, and it still takes a village. It took me raising my hand and asking for help.

"Hey, hubby, can you help watch the kids this weekend so I can get some work done?"

"Hey, Instagram friends, can you share this in your social

media feeds to let people know about this book I wrote called *Party Girl*?"

"Hey, manager at work, I can meet all of your priorities, but not without another team member or an extension on the due date. I'm only one person."

When I wanted to train for a half marathon, I asked someone on Dave's team at work if he could coach me. The only thing I knew about him was that he was a marathon runner. Ken taught me everything I know about running long distance.

When I wanted to write that first book, my mom came to town many, many weekends and helped with the boys so I could write. She would show up in our upstairs bedroom with snacks at almost the exact moment I was ready to throw the computer against the wall.

When this company I've built started to scale so big and so fast that I didn't think I could properly run it alone anymore, I swallowed a massive amount of ego and asked my husband for help. Do you know how much pride I had being a female founder and CEO with a high school education? A lot. Do you know how interested I was in admitting to him, to myself, or to you that I couldn't continue to lead the company and lead this tribe simultaneously? Not interested at all. But the thing is, I've learned over the last decade how easy it is to burn out—or worse—give up on your dream because you're trying to do too many things at once. So I've learned. And I ask for help.

I have help, you guys. I have so much dang help, and I'm always looking for ways to free up more of my time so I can focus on my values.

People ask me all the time how I "do it all," and I am happy to shout it from the rooftops. I don't!

We have a full-time nanny, and we've had one since our oldest was three months old. Because of moves or additional kids added to our family, we've had three separate nannies (though not all at once) in our history as a family. These women—Martha, Jojo, and now Angie—have loved my children well and made it possible for me to pursue my career while Dave pursued his. They came in early and stayed late. They allowed us to have weekly date nights and, occasionally, they stayed the night so we could get away. We have never had family nearby who could help with our children, and these women were our surrogate family. I can't imagine how we would have managed without them.

Three years ago we hired a housekeeper. Full-time. We talked about and planned for years to get to the place financially where we could afford a full-time housekeeper, and it's the greatest luxury in our life! The more kids we had, the less we wanted to spend our nights and weekends doing laundry and mopping floors. We also craved help with dinners and grocery shopping and someone who would take our minivan or our mini schnauzer to get washed.

I have an assistant at work as well as a team of people at the Hollis Company who support me in my business endeavors. I use stylists to pick out flattering outfits for me when I go to fancy red-carpet events or on TV shows. I use hair and makeup people when I'm going to be on television, and a few times I've had a woman come to my home and give me a spray tan in my bathroom. She had a pop-up tent; I thought it was magical!

If this much help seems excessive, I'd challenge you to weigh it against the level of content we've been able to push out into the world over the last five years. I wouldn't have been able to do a tenth of this work if I hadn't had help. If this much help seems unnecessary, well dang, sis, you don't have to go full tilt like I do, but please teach yourself to raise your hand and admit where you're struggling!

You don't need to be in a specific financial place to get help: you can trade with a friend or simply ask your partner for more support. You *do need* to be in a specific emotional place to get help; you do need to realize that while you are blazing a new trail for yourself, you aren't required to walk down it alone.

The point in all of this long and crazy rant is that if you struggle with admitting that you need help, you have to take a good hard look at what is required to get you to the next level. If there's a time commitment involved and you already feel like you don't have enough time, you might need to ask for help. If there's a level of knowledge involved that you don't already have, you might need to find a teacher. If there's a promotional level involved, you might need to ask your existing customers if they'd be willing to help you get it out in the world.

I heard once that most people who choke to death on food do it in close proximity to someone who could have saved them. It's a horrible reality. What happens is that they're sitting at a table eating with a group, and when they begin to choke they feel embarrassed that they're struggling. Inevitably they stand up from the table, and when their friends ask if they're okay or need help, they wave them away like everything's fine. They go to another room so their struggle won't be a bother to anyone. It's not until they're alone and really fighting for breath that they realize they need assistance, but by then it's too late.

Friends, your struggles don't mean that you're weak; they mean you're human. Your inexperience doesn't mean you won't succeed; it just means you haven't yet. Stop pretending. Stop faking it. Stop suffering in silence. Stop setting yourself up as a martyr. Stop taking it all on alone and then feeling bitter about it. Stop wasting your time on activities you hate as penance for the time you want for yourself.

You cannot do enough loads of laundry to make your husband support your dream. You cannot volunteer enough hours at church to make your sister understand your goals. You cannot earn your way to autonomy over your own life—it's a human right you were granted when you became an adult. If you need to, *when you need to*, raise your hand and ask for help, regardless of what anyone else thinks about it.

There are a hundred ways to learn to swim and one very easy way to drown, and that is by being unwilling to admit you're drowning in the first place.

BEHAVIOR 5:

BUILD FOUNDATIONS FOR SUCCESS

I spent years talking to women about how to reach for growth without realizing that many of them didn't have a strong foundation to keep up with their goals even if they were motivated. The truth is, it doesn't matter if you're motivated to achieve a goal if your day-to-day life is going to sabotage you before you get very far. This lack of foundation wasn't even something I put a name to until I started to dig into the reasons women would list for why they were having so much trouble. The things we need in place before we can pursue our dreams are not what we often think of in relation to success. Typically, we just think of them as parts of life. But if we don't have these foundational elements squared away on the front end, reaching for anything else can feel like too much of a long shot.

We have to do the necessary initial work if we're going to move forward in other ways. We need to set ourselves up to win.

Think about it this way. You're like a vase. I heard this one time, and I thought this was the greatest analogy ever. Imagine that you are a glass vase and you're standing up tall, and someone is pouring water into you. That water is everything you could possibly need to survive. So you, as the glass vase, are filled with life and energy and nutrients and love and joy—all the good things.

But we women often don't think about ourselves as much as we worry about everyone else, so we try and lean over. We tip our vases forward and backward and side to side so that the good things we're receiving will spill out to those around us. We give some to our children, or our coworkers, or our parents, or our friends. We keep tipping ourselves over. We tip it a little bit here, we spill a little bit there, and eventually . . . the vase falls over and breaks into a thousand pieces. We spend so much effort trying to take care of others that we destroy ourselves in the process.

But here's the incredible thing. If you're a vase and you just stand up tall and proud on a firm foundation, if you just take in all the things that are being poured into you, what will eventually happen to the water in the vase? It will overflow and spill out to everyone around you.

I know this is one of those things we hear all the time, and you're like, "Yeah, I got it."

I'm here to tell you, no, you don't got it. You don't! I'm challenging you right now. If you are uncomfortable, if you are aching, if you are tired, if you are anxious, if you are depressed, if you are suffering in any way, you're not standing firmly on a strong foundation and letting your vase overflow. You're not setting yourself up for success. But you can. And here are some tangible steps you can take to do just that.

GET HEALTHY

I can't think of anything that's as important to ensure success as feeling great both physically and emotionally. It's certainly possible to achieve a goal even when you're not operating at the highest level, but it's way harder than it needs to be. You can drive with a flat tire, but when the car is fine-tuned and the gas tank is full, you can fly. Over the last decade I've worked so hard to get physically and emotionally healthy, and while the road from there to here was filled with personal awareness and hard work (and gobs of therapy), there are a handful of practical things I've identified as game changers for health that you, too, can implement. These are the five things I changed in my life over the years that made me feel physically capable of taking on all my big dreams. These are the "Five to Thrive" elements I mentioned earlier.

1. Hydration

Drink half your body weight in ounces of water every single day. Let's do easy math. Let's say you weigh a hundred pounds. You're going to divide that in half—that's fifty. So you should drink fifty ounces of water every single day to stay hydrated. At this point I always get asked the same question: Doesn't that mean you have to pee all day? Yes, that's the point. It flushes all the bad stuff out of your body.

Hydration is important for so many reasons, but it's especially important for those of you who are struggling with weight loss. Being dehydrated feels a lot like being hungry. Chances are you're not hungry; you're thirsty. But your brain doesn't know the difference, which is why you're struggling so much with portion control. Try drinking a bottle of water and then seeing if you still need food.

Or, you might be like, "I want this goal. I want this plan. I want to have a better life. I want to get promoted. I want to do this." But you don't have the energy, and you keep giving up on your dreams, and nothing seems to be working. You don't understand why, but you also haven't had water since last Tuesday—and that was only because some got in your mouth when you were brushing your teeth.

Hydration is one of those foundational elements for success, so whenever someone wants to start a new plan, whatever it may be, I always recommend they begin with this little step. Just drink your water, and once you tackle that and make it a habit, you'll feel ready to move on to tougher things.

2. Wake Up Earlier

The second thing that you're going to do as you establish a healthier physical environment is get up an hour earlier and use that time for yourself. I think this is especially powerful for those of you who are moms. I know I shouldn't make sweeping generalizations about other people's families, but I'm going to stand firm in this idea.

If your kid wakes you up in the morning, you're screwed. You are. You're already behind the eight ball. If the baby is crying or a toddler woke you up asking for Cheerios, you're starting your day on the defensive instead of on the offensive. That extra hour in the morning before your family gets up is key; it's everything.

Those of you who say you don't have any time for yourself, this is the time! If you want to work out, if you want to read a book, if you want to pray, if you want to write your first novel, if you want to have the time to pursue your goals, get up an hour earlier.

Now, inevitably, when I talk about waking up earlier I always get a few notes from women saying something along the lines of, "I have a six-week-old baby and I'm struggling to wake up an hour earlier because I only got two hours of sleep last night."

What are you talking about right now? What in the holy world?! If you have a baby under nine months of age, this number on the list is not meant for you! Just wait until they're older and then try. Be gracious with yourself. I love that you're trying to push yourself into something new, but these are not adjustments you can make if you are currently going through a massive life change. So if you've got a new baby, this one is not for you.

Maybe what you're thinking instead is, *I'm a doctor, and I get up at 3:00 a.m. already.* Well, gosh, I definitely don't want you to be up at 2:00 a.m. But maybe for you this step looks like finding some time for yourself later in the day. Come on, friend. We're just looking to carve out an hour of time somewhere to pursue what's on your heart. That's all I want you to do.

If you don't have an hour to spare, you don't have a life.

I piss people off when I say that. They're like, "You don't know me! You don't know my schedule!" You're right. I don't know you. But what I do know is that if you can't find a single hour for *yourself* in a twenty-four-hour period, you need to look at your priorities. You need to ask yourself what you are doing with your time.

3. Give Up *One* Category of Food for Thirty Days

So, we're going to drink water, we're going to get up an hour earlier, and then we're going to focus on nutrition with this easy elimination. I want you to give up food. One category of crappy food, for thirty days. Have you ever heard that saying that if you can give up something for a month, it becomes a habit? Well, I want you to make a habit of not eating garbage. Garbage in this instance is fast food or processed food or anything Krispy Kreme makes! And the thing is, I don't even want you to give up everything or figure out a new diet, because that can be overwhelming, particularly if you're also trying to chase down a goal. I just want you to choose one tiny baby category . . . and then avoid it like a biblical plague.

If you can give something up—like truly give it up, no "cheating" —it becomes a habit. I hate to say the word *cheat,* but if you break this promise to yourself, it's done. It won't stick. For most things in life, if you mess up, I'm likely to simply say, "Get back up, get back up, get back up." But if you can't stick on this number, you've got to start again at the beginning of your thirty days.

The challenge to you is, Can you keep a promise to yourself for a month? I don't even care if you replace it with something else. I don't care if you're like, "Well, I can't have Diet Coke, so I'm going to have lemonade—which is full of sugar, but whatever, at least it's not full of chemicals!" This isn't about what you're giving up; this is about proving to yourself that you can keep your word. And proving to your stomach that it can in fact survive without Chick-fil-A sauce for an extended period of time.

4. Move Your Body Every Day!

So you're going to drink water, you're going to wake up an hour earlier, you're going to give up a category of food for thirty days, and you are going to move your body. No, you don't have to do CrossFit or sign up for a boot camp where they scream at you for an hour. I mean, unless that's your thing. But you do need to move your body for thirty minutes every single day. And let me say this right now, if you cannot find the time and the energy and the willpower to move your body for thirty minutes a day, seven days a week, we have a problem. We have a really big problem. I'm not asking you to run a marathon; I'm asking you to move.

I know that there are a hundred million distractions that encourage you to lie around and watch television or scroll through your phone, but if that's the only thing you do in your downtime, you're depleting yourself of energy. You don't have to be a certain size or a certain weight, but you do have to have energy. You are a freaking animal. An animal, like a cheetah or an antelope or a wolverine. There are no overweight animals in nature; it's not a thing.

The only overweight animals that exist are the ones that live in our houses with us. Animals are not overweight; pets are overweight. You are not a pet. You are a powerful, beautiful, bold woman, and you will treat yourself as such.

Studies have been done on the highest performers, the people who are the greatest athletes, the greatest businesswomen, the greatest in the world. Out of the highest-performing people, it's something like 97 percent—I swear, you can look this up—who work out at least five days a week. It's not because those people were given some special workout genes that you don't have. It's because those people know that energy begets energy. You want to achieve your goal? Get moving for those thirty minutes every day, and make sure your body is ready to act on the vision you have for your life.

5. Practice Gratitude Daily

The fifth thing I want you to do is arguably the most important. Every single day I'm going to ask you to write down ten things you are grateful for. Put it in your phone, write it down in a journal, however you want to do it, but take twelve minutes and list these things out. Don't list big things, like that you're grateful for your partner or that you're grateful for the ability to breathe. Write down things that happened today. Things like how good your cup of coffee was. Or how someone let you in on the freeway when there was heavy traffic. Or that you got to see a friend, or that your five-year-old told you a terrible joke and you laughed even though it wasn't funny. The idea is, if you know that at the end of the day you're going to have to list out points of gratitude, you will spend your day looking for blessings. If you spend your day looking for blessings—here's the magic—you'll find them.

When you live your life in a state of gratitude, it changes everything. From a place of feeling immensely blessed, we see immense possibility; we believe good things are possible and maybe even likely to happen to us. When it comes to setting the foundation to succeed, it helps if you believe that your success is likely. If you don't do anything else on this list, just do this one thing.

If you don't feel like you can do all five things, just try that last one about gratitude and do it consistently for a month. I suggest a month because in my own life I've found that if I can do anything regularly for thirty days, it sticks. When you practice gratitude consistently for a month, add in the water, then maybe the workout. This is about setting yourself up for success. You can certainly pursue your goals when you're struggling physically or emotionally, but when you're taking care of yourself, you have the exponential energy to keep up with your vision.

GET YOUR PERSONAL SPACE IN ORDER

Being a little girl in a house that was at times utter chaos meant that I grew up often feeling unsafe. But the one thing that I could control was my bed. So I made my bed every single day. When I grew up and got my first apartment, it was in a crappy part of town. In fact, it was actually a crappy apartment in a crappy part of town, but that apartment was always clean. This was something I could control.

Your home is something you can control. Of all the things in your life it's the one you have the easiest access to. Years ago I was watching *The Oprah Winfrey Show*, and she said, "Your home should rise up to meet you." If your home feels like chaos or it's dirty or it's unorganized, you need to wake up. If you keep scrolling through Instagram, looking at other women's pretty lives so you don't have to acknowledge that yours is a mess, you need to wake up. Your home is a reflection of what's going on inside your head and your heart. If life feels out of control, start taking control with your immediate environment.

I know there are people reading this who don't have a home, who don't have access to everything, who have one tiny square surrounded by a sea of chaos. To you, I'd say, take care of the spaces that are yours, be that your bed, your car, or your desk at work. Organize your life. Keep your spaces clean. Put some effort into their appearances. These things are about self-respect and about setting a certain standard for yourself, for your life, for your children. That doesn't cost money. Self-respect doesn't cost anything other than effort. Clean up.

The other thing to keep in mind about your personal spaces is that they not only need to be organized and clean, but they need to be filled with reminders of the vision you have for your future life. When I open up my closet doors, I have bulletin boards with pictures pinned that reflect my bigger vision for the future, because I want to remind myself every day what I'm working toward. I use images and words; my car and office and even my bathroom mirror are filled with words and quotes that inspire me. This entire chapter is about setting yourself up to reach for success by building a solid foundation. The spaces you inhabit can be the platform that you build a new life on, or they can be the anchor that keeps pulling you back under the waves.

BUILD A GREAT COMMUNITY

You are a combination of the five people you hang out with most. Think about it. Who do you see most often? Whose words are you consuming frequently? Which points of view and perceptions do you take in on the regular? Is there someone amongst those five you interact with regularly who is above you in life? Meaning, is there something about them that you want to aspire to? Do they have skills or characteristics that you'd be proud to adopt? When you hang out with those people, is there an area in your life that they're going to pull you up toward?

If you're the smartest person in the room, you're in the wrong room. If you're the most focused on growth in your group of friends, if you're the highest achiever, if you're the most compassionate, if you're doing the best out of everyone, you're in the wrong room. You should want to surround yourself with people who are better than you in the areas you want to improve in. You should hope that your good stuff rubs off on them and their good stuff rubs off on you. But if everyone in your circle looks to you to motivate them, you're outnumbered. They're much more likely to pull you down to their level than you are to pull them up to yours.

It's worth saying here that I'm not suggesting that you let go of the relationships that you have simply because someone isn't as advanced as you are or as focused on growth. I *am* suggesting that you make sure you are regularly interacting with people who are leading the charge in an area you'd like to grow into.

I want to hang out with other women or other couples who exemplify the traits I would want to have as a mom, as a wife, as a woman in business, and as a friend. If you want to grow in your career but all your friends are still living at home with no plans to do much with their lives, how supportive are they able to be? If your friends—the ones who advise you and offer counsel—don't believe in marriage, how much great advice are they going to offer you for yours?

I remember one summer we were on a vacation in Hawaii, and it was during a really rough season in our marriage. I went into the vacation already feeling frustrated with Dave, and that much time together only brought it into sharper relief. I was so annoyed with him that it colored every part of that vacation. About halfway through the trip some of my best friends came to visit us, and I went to pick them up from the airport. I had been waiting for days, thinking, *Great, my girls are coming, and I'm going to unload on what a terrible human this man is and they're going to be like, yes, screw him!* Plus, they're lesbians, so I figured they'd be even more into the whole "husbands are the worst!" diatribe I had going on in my head. I had a whole plan!

Then we got into the car where I started making known all my frustrations. Bless—seriously, God bless—these women, because they immediately started speaking truth into what I would want for a marriage. They reminded me what grace looks like and that we all have hard times. They reminded me that when things are the toughest, that's when you should most be seeking out your partner. They reminded me who it is I want to be.

Now, if I had gotten into a car with best friends who were people with a totally opposite view on what it is to have a strong and beautiful marriage, we would have gotten out of that car in a totally different headspace. They would have fanned the flames of my anger. They would have made the situation worse. It would have been so easy to do.

Are your friends pulling you up or dragging you down?

You are a combination of the five people that you hang out with most. Choose wisely.

DEVELOP GREAT HABITS

In order to get from where I was to where I wanted to be, I had to learn about habits. I had to learn to change the bad habits I had been practicing, and I had to learn how to develop the good habits I needed to get ahead. So many people think that one thing, one opportunity, is going to make them a success at everything. The reality is that success comes by doing fifty things over and over and over and over. Intensity is not as important as consistency. The thing about consistency is that you do it for a while, and it seems like nothing is happening. Nothing's happening, nothing's happening, and then all of a sudden you're like, *Holy crap, where did that come from?!*

What habits do you have right now that are going to help you get to where you want to go? Having a good life is about developing good habits. But what exactly is a habit? A habit is a series of three things:

1. A cue
2. An action
3. A reward

A cue means that something happens. It's a trigger for you. It signals to your brain that it's time to start the action. Then, when you take the action (totally unconsciously, by the way), you're given some type of reward. A cue, an activity, a reward.

For instance, I spent many years as an emotional eater. When you're an emotional eater, every single kind of emotion is a cue to eat something. If you're sad you eat. If you're happy you eat. If you're anxious you should eat. If you're mad you should eat, and then you should have Oreos. I had learned somewhere along the way that food was the only thing I had easy access to that would make me feel better. So, when I became an adult, whenever I had anxiety or fear, I would go to the kitchen at eleven o'clock at night and binge eat everything.

My cue was feeling anxious, my activity was eating, and the reward was that I felt better. For a brief period of time, I would get a high from eating all that food, and that high made me feel happy. But the problem with most terrible habits is that, as the high from your reward starts to die off, it actually triggers the cue again. So for me, I would eat an entire sleeve of Ritz crackers and half a tub of cream cheese, and it would make me so happy. Then twenty minutes would go by and I'd start thinking, *You're a piece of crap! You blew your diet. You've been working so hard, and you just threw it all away. You're garbage.* The negative self-talk would start, and then I'd think, *Well, dang. We're already here; let's have dessert.* And then I would eat dessert and feel really good again, but eventually circle back around.

I would trigger myself again and again and again, until I finally understood that the issue wasn't stress; the issue was the activity I was unconsciously choosing once the stress had been cued. I couldn't change that life was going to happen and that there would be times when I would feel scared or sad or anxious. What I could change, however, was the action I took in response to that cue.

Now, when I have anxiety, I go on a long run. I go work out. By the way, I used to hate people who are like, "If you feel stressed, go work out." I'd think, *Screw you, Pam! We're not all made like that, okay?!* Except neither is Pam. She's just choosing a better activity to manage what she's feeling. She's taught herself a great habit.

The equation for change in any capacity is always very simple. For example, it's so simple to lose weight. It is so simple to get in shape. It's so simple to save money. It's all very, very simple, but it's not easy. It's not quick. It's not a reward that you're going to get immediately. You usually have to choose a harder thing where the reward comes later. The problem with most things in life is that the activity you *want* to do—the bad habit—offers a quicker reward than the thing that's better for you.

It's difficult to make a change because the bad choices are much easier to access than the good ones. You've created a habit of bad habits. They feel more natural to you. Whatever you're reading this book for: maybe you needed to get in shape, maybe you wanted to eat better, maybe you wanted to be more intentional with your partner, maybe you wanted to be a better mom, maybe you wanted to be calmer, maybe you wanted to battle your anxiety, or your depression, or to replace your depression with gratitude and joy. Maybe you wanted to reach for all those things. But maybe you have a year, or a decade, or a lifetime of habitually being angry, pushing people away, binge eating, abusing alcohol, ignoring your kids, being a workaholic. You have your own version; you fill in the blank. Maybe this makes you think you can't swap out the good actions for the bad ones, but I know for a fact that if you're breathing right now, if you're alive, that means you can start again. You can start again over and over and over until the feeling of moving in the right direction is more natural to you than the feeling of giving up. Whatever it is that you are facing, whatever your struggle is, whatever your hill is to climb, whatever you are trying to get through, there are ways to take ownership of that thing, and you can do it as you come back one day at a time and establish consistency.

ESTABLISH A MORNING ROUTINE

The last thing I want us to talk about to set ourselves up for success is the ever-important morning routine. I know we discussed this earlier in the chapter, but it's such an important part of laying a solid foundation that I'd like us to spend a little more time on this and dig in deeper. It's hard to believe that having a good morning is such a key factor to setting yourself up for success, but it really is. I don't think I understood this until I had children. Before I had kids, the morning was my own. I decided when I wanted to wake up. I decided what I wanted to do with that time. I never once opened my eyes and saw a toddler staring at me like a creepy extra from *Children of the Corn*! But then I had kids, and suddenly someone else was dictating my mornings, which I suppose would be fine if I had been one of those well-organized mothers who manage to make parenting look effortless. But our reality was often messy and chaotic and hard and frustrating. We'd survive (barely), and I would get the kids off to school. But because the morning was chaotic and frustrating, I was starting almost every workday feeling chaotic and frustrated. It was hard to shake.

It wasn't until I started the practice of waking up an hour before my children that I understood how powerful it is to get ahead of the day. Now, I am intentionally planning my morning routine around the kind of day I want to have, because if you own the morning, then you own the day. If you own the day, then you own the week. It's the ultimate routine you can set for yourself, and mine is made up of practices I've worked and reworked hundreds of times to get to the ultimate start to my days. I'm sharing it with you now to give you a head start on creating one for yourself.

1. **I wake up at 5:00 a.m.** Our kids typically wake up at 6:45, so I used to get up at 5:45 to give myself an hour of "me time." But then I realized having only one hour of me time made me feel a little rushed. I really like the ritual of a slow cup of coffee in the morning, and I don't want to rush through it. So now I wake up at 5:00 a.m. and go turn on the

coffeepot (someday I'll learn how to program that stupid thing). I drink a glass of water while the coffee brews, and then I start working on my current project, whatever that may be. I like working on big projects early in the morning because I'm generally not awake enough to second-guess myself, which means I make a lot more progress.

2. **After I finish my morning work, I do a fifteen-minute meditation on gratitude.** If you've never done meditation before, think of it as guided prayer. And, in my case, I use the time to focus on my blessings so I start my day aware of all the things that I have to be grateful for.

3. **Next, I write in my journal.** This is a really quick habit of writing down my intentions for the day, a few things I'm grateful for, and an affirmation reminding me who I want to be.

4. **Once I have gotten some things accomplished, had my coffee, and mentally prepared myself to be my best, it's time to wake up the hellions who live down the hall.** The next hour of our day is all about the kids. This is when we do breakfast, brush teeth, get dressed for school, make lunches, and get everyone out the door.

5. **After the kids are at school, I hurry to get ready for work and always, always, always get ready to upbeat music.** I absolutely love music, and I use it constantly to pump me up and get me going. I have an Amazon Echo in my bathroom, so I can voice command it to play anything at any point. I love that I can be in the shower and be like,

"Alexa, play 'Shake It Off' by Taylor Swift," and two seconds later I'm jamming out to Tay Tay.

6. **Once I'm ready for work, I head back to the kitchen to make my green smoothie.** It is not delicious or exciting, but it's full of a ton of stuff that's really good for me, it keeps me full for hours, and starting my day in a healthy way sets the tone for the hours that come after.

7. **The last thing I do as part of my morning routine is write down my list of ten dreams and the one goal that's going to get me there fastest.** 10, 10, 1, remember? It's a great way to set my focus before I start on my to-do list, and I love that I have an entire notebook filled with things that remind me who it is I want to be.

BEHAVIOR 6:

STOP ALLOWING THEM TO TALK YOU OUT OF IT

Have you ever experienced a situation where you were motivated and inspired and ready to push forward toward your goal? Maybe you were devoted to your weight-loss journey and were making great strides. Maybe you decided to go back to school. Maybe you were training for that half marathon. Whatever it was, you were on it. And then . . . then someone else got in your way.

This can manifest in a lot of ways for hundreds of reasons, but often it looks something like this: You are doing great on your diet, but then you go to a family gathering and someone in your family (or maybe several someones) gives you grief about it. *But it's a special occasion! But it's Christmas! But we always have margaritas—what, you're just not going to drink now?* And the thing is, staying on your diet during a family party or a holiday is really, really tough. So, when they give you a hard time (at best) or tease you mercilessly (at worst), you allow the emotions they evoke in you to talk you into breaking your diet.

Or maybe you're training for your first race or you've decided to go back to school to get your master's degree, and at first the people in your life are supportive. Going back to school is a good thing. Working out and getting in shape are great. Everyone around you agrees. But then you start to schedule time in your calendar to work on these things, and as the race ramps up, you've got to spend more and more hours training. Or maybe it's studying or writing a report for class. The free time you used to have is now devoted to your new goal. And the people in your life feel left out or left behind or, more typically, inconvenienced. These choices you're making for yourself feel more and more self-ish, and someone in your life speaks into that. "You know, it's really hard to handle the kids all by myself on Thursdays while you're at class." Or, "We used to always hang out, and I feel like I never see you anymore!" You were already feeling guilty about your choices and it is getting harder by the day, so you bow to whatever would make everyone else happy. God forbid they might be upset with you! It's so much better to give up on your thing, your goal, because if anyone else is inconvenienced, then your goal must be wrong.

Can we talk about that for a quick second? Can we talk about someone else being inconvenienced by you pursuing your best self? I want to bring it up because it's a question I get a lot.

How can I get my mom to be more supportive?

How do I convince my husband to watch the kids so I can work out?

How can I get my boyfriend to eat healthy with me so it's eas-ier for me to stay on track?

How can I get my dad to support my decision to change majors?

The best advice I know of in this situation is, if you want to change someone else, change yourself. People change because they're inspired by someone else's example, not because they were coerced into doing it. People change because they see in someone else what's probable, not because someone harasses them over and over about what's possible. You will never change someone else unless you find the courage and the will and the resolve to change yourself, and you will never do any of those things if you aren't willing to let people be inconvenienced by your journey.

Being inconvenienced is part of any relationship. I will watch all four kids by myself for a couple of hours on Saturday so that Dave can go to the gym. He will watch all four kids by himself on Sunday so that I can go on a long run. Is it an inconvenience to solo parent that many beasties? Of course, but we both genuinely want the best for each other, and that means we're willing to do things that are hard on us so our partner can flourish. How many people work extra hours for years while their partner gets their degree? How many times have you done the grocery shopping? How many times has your partner taken the trash out or done the laundry or gotten up with the baby to make it easier on you? Being occasionally inconvenienced is a part of life, and if you're willing to do it for them, then you better be willing to demand that they do it for you.

Sometimes all it takes is having a firm adult conversation. But sometimes the pushback is hard to stand strong against. It's inevitable that the people in your life will feel the discomfort that arises when you start restructuring your life to pursue new things. There are so many reasons why your friends or family members might not be supportive: insecurity, fear, self-preservation, complacency, and so on. But this book isn't about their reasons; it's about *you* having a revelation. So listen up. Mediocre will always try and drag you back down to mediocre. Lazy will always try and drag you back down to lazy.

For whatever reason, these people in your life aren't at the same place as you in their personal-growth journey, and that's fine. We're all on our own paths, and it's not your job to try and pull them up with you. It's *your job* to show up for *your own life* and fight for your own dreams. To quote my friend Elizabeth, "You need less wishbone and more backbone."

That means you're going to have to make the decision that other people don't get to weigh in here. That means you will stand up for yourself and understand that someone who's sitting in the cheap seats doesn't get to tell you how to fight in the ring. If you're not out here on the field, if you're not fighting for more, if you're not running these miles with me or writing these words with me or making new habits with me or eating this kale with me—if you're not in the game with me, then you don't get to call any plays, and you darn sure don't get to offer negative comments about the work I'm putting in!

Allowing someone else to talk you out of your pursuits is quite possibly one of the hardest habits to break but one of the greatest behaviors to adopt. Part of what makes it hard is that we care about what other people think; it's ingrained in us from birth. But, as we've talked about before, other people's opinions of you are none of your business. That's a bit harder to remember, though, when the opinions—even when they're wrong—are connected to the people we love and care about most. The thing is, you cannot control how they'll act or what they'll say or whether they'll be supportive. You can only control how you'll respond to what they do and whether you use their feelings as a reason to quit on yourself. Rather than alienate everyone or start a turf war with your sister or create problems in your relationships, here are some things you can do to ensure that you're better able to control your own reactions:

1. ASK YOURSELF IF THIS PERSON SHOULD BE IN YOUR LIFE—SERIOUSLY.

Think about it for a second. If someone doesn't want what's best for you—even if they don't understand it—it's either because y'all have a problem you need to work through or they shouldn't be in your life. You either want to do life with people (meaning interact with them happily), or you shouldn't have them in your life. Period. I know this seems almost blasphemous to some people, but you really, truly don't have to hang out with people who are negative or mean or make you anxious or bring out the worst in you. Even family. There are whole groups of blood relatives I haven't interacted with since I became an adult. As a child I didn't have a choice, but as an adult I decided I wouldn't ever allow people into my home and around my children who were mean or prone to creating drama or passive-aggressively bullying others. That's not the way we behave, and though it makes me sad because I miss the good times we had, I'm not willing to allow the bad times in order to be invited to the annual summer barbecue. Be kind or leave. That's our motto, and if you can't abide by it, then you're not the type of person I want in my life.

2. PREPARE BEFORE YOU SEE THEM.

More often than not, the answer isn't to cut someone out of your life. More often than not you can recognize that they've got some insecurities and decide not to let it affect you. But if you wait until you're in front of your naysayer to decide how to respond to them, you're screwed. That's like being on a diet and waiting until you're starving to figure out what to eat. You've got a zero-percent chance of being the person you want to be if you're not intentional about it. Hope is not a strategy, remember? So the next time you're headed into a scenario where you'll likely interact with people who aren't supportive, ask yourself in advance how you can circumnavigate it.

Please note that I didn't say *avoid it*. Heading to Thanksgiving with a plan to drink as much pinot as possible to numb yourself to their comments is not an effective strategy. Believe me, I know from personal experience. Instead, ask yourself what is likely to come up. Steel yourself for the comments and have your responses ready to go. Know your why. Remind yourself what you're doing this for and why it matters so much to you. Prepare yourself physically. Listen to some great pump-up music to get you in the right headspace, and decide that this experience and interaction is going to be fantastic because you won't allow it to be anything else. If the interaction will be difficult because it has to do with diet or health or exercise, consider eating or working out or whatever you need to do before you interact. That way it's already done.

A few years ago I became a pescetarian, and when I went to family parties there often wasn't much I could eat. People noticed my mostly empty plate, which led to lots of comments and teasing about "going LA on us." Many times I'd buckle and eat something I didn't want to eat but leave the party frustrated and annoyed. I needed to prepare myself for a more successful interaction with people who might not understand my choices. Now I just make a big salad and a great veggie side dish for every family party. This way I've got something to eat that's on my diet, and my plate is full, so no one questions what is or isn't there. Also, my salads are bomb, so everybody wins.

3. PLAN INTENTIONALLY TO MAKE IT EASIER.

I wish this section was as easy as telling you to have the people in your life get with the program and stop acting like unsupportive punks. But, dude, it's not that easy. It wasn't that easy in my marriage or with my family, so I know it won't be that easy for your relationships either. Whenever I'm about to take on a new project or I've got a particularly busy season, I map it out in advance to make it as easy as possible on Dave. I plan for sitters, I figure out workarounds, I schedule like a maniac to make my hustle as little of an inconvenience as possible. Ultimately, though, working on your own goal typically means sacrificing in another area of your life.

It means your partner is going to have to put the kids to bed on the nights you're at school. It means you can't join your girl-friends for Taco Tuesday anymore because you're committed to your health. It means time and energy focused in on the thing you're working for, which means less of those things other people may have come to expect. Talk to your partner and your friends and anyone whose opinion does matter to you. Tell them your why and your how, and work together to find alternatives for the must-haves that won't be able to happen exactly as they did before. If you've done everything you can do to make the transition easy and fair for your loved ones, you'll be better prepared to manage the guilt when it starts to creep up to rob you of motivation.

BEHAVIOR 7:

LEARN TO SAY NO

I recognize this may make me a pariah in certain social circles, but I'm going to go ahead and say it anyway.

I don't volunteer at my kids' school.

Not because I don't have time. My calendar is packed, but I'm in control of it. I could make time. And not because there isn't opportunity to do it, because I get the requests to sign up for craft day or the field trip to Underwood Family Farms just like every other parent. No, I don't volunteer at my children's school, because . . . I hate it. Shoot! I know I'm going to get angry notes about this, but I've got to be honest. It's my nightmare.

For years and years I signed up to volunteer. I was room mom. I stuffed the Thursday folders. I planned the parties and herded children through the pumpkin patch during the fall field trip. And I hated every single part of it, except for getting to hang out with my kid during a weekday.

Moms are supposed to want to hang out at school, right? They're supposed to want to volunteer. They're supposed to love every single child on the planet, especially everyone in their kid's second-grade class.

But I don't.

Some of those kids on the field trips, they're the worst. You know it's true! And stuffing Thursday folders is so boring I want to lie down and die right on top of that half-circle table they make you sit at in a chair made for an eight-year-old!

I dislike it all. Immensely.

Now, just so we're clear, I'll do it if it needs to be done. I faithfully showed up to two years of preschool board meetings. I worked the snack bar at the winter festival and planned the annual fundraiser for our local elementary school. Why? Because there was nobody else to do it, and I will totally take one for the team if it needs to be done.

But, if there are eighty-seven other parents who love volunteering and they're wondering would Ford's mom like to sign up for classroom-helper day this quarter? Nope. No, thank you.

Years ago Jen Hatmaker reminded us of this quote, "If it's not a *hell yes*, it's a no."[1] Meaning, if someone asks you to do something outside of your regularly scheduled programming and your immediate gut reaction isn't "Hell, yes!" then you should absolutely say, "No, thank you."

Volunteering at school isn't my jam, and unless there's some kind of shortage on helpers, I'm not going to commit to it. It gets me all kinds of side-eyes and snarky comments from the other moms at school, and I promise you, *promise*, that someone somewhere (maybe many someones) just read that I don't like to volunteer and got pissed. They decided right here and now—based on that single statement—that I'm a bad mom.

You are never, ever supposed to admit you don't like certain parts of parenting. It's an unspoken rule. Not volunteering at school? I can imagine impassioned readers shaking their fists at the sky. *What kind of monster doesn't want to help America's youth? What kind of jerk can't commit to an hour a week helping out in the classroom? You need to get your priorities straight, sister!*

Here's the thing, though. My priorities are super straight. Here they are:

- Myself, my personal growth, and my faith.
- My husband and our commitment to an exceptional marriage.
- My children and my commitment to be an exceptional mother.
- My work and larger mission to give women the tools to change their lives.

I'm sure there's some confusion here, because I've listed out being an exceptional mother and yet I'm admitting that I won't volunteer at my kids' school. Well, here is the power of being extremely clear on your priorities and how they manifest according to you. I personally don't believe that I need to volunteer at their school to be a good mom. You may absolutely believe you do in your own life—and that's awesome because it'll give you some guidance on how to lay out your own wills and won'ts—but for me, volunteering doesn't equal parental success. Cheering at sporting events, sitting for hours during the school musical, regularly having family dinners and family vacations, taking the kids on business trips so they get alone time with me, reading bedtime stories, tucking them in at night—these are just a handful of things that are sacrosanct to me as a mom. These are just a few of my *hell yes* moments when it comes to parenting. These are what I'm committed to do no matter what, but to make sure I have time to get to all the things on my priorities list (not just my children), I've got to be crystal clear about what matters to me and to them.

Notice that nowhere on the list did I write out, "Make sure the other moms at school approve of me." Or, "Live life to meet other people's expectations and priorities." I don't have the time or the energy for that. I've decided on four areas of focus for my life, and if the activity I've been invited to take part in doesn't serve one of those four things, then I can't do it. Remember, if everything is important then nothing is. If everything demands your attention, you'll never have focus. If you allow other people to dictate your schedule to you, they absolutely will.

I've learned to say no.

More than that, I've learned to say no without even one second of guilt or shame about it, and I can tell you that it's magic! I get to live life in a way that makes sense for my family, and I promise you we are all better off for it. My kids get more dedicated time in the areas that matter to us, and I'm not running through life exhausted and overextended.

Have you learned to say no yet? Do you need to? Here is my best advice for how to teach yourself this practice:

RESPOND ASAP

To stay organized in business, you're told to "only touch something once." Meaning, if you open an email you respond to it then. If you take a meeting, you come up with a plan of action while you're in the room. Only touch it once. Well, this needs to apply to requests for your time as well: only touch it once in that, as soon as you get the request, you respond as soon as possible in the affirmative or the negative. No *maybe*s or *probably*s. *Maybe* and *probably* is code for "I really don't want to do this, but I don't want to tell you that." You likely won't suddenly develop the courage later to tell whoever's asking that you're not interested. Instead, you'll sit on it until it's too late to cancel and end up doing this thing you didn't actually want to do.

That's how you become Bitter Barbie. When someone asks you for something, go with your gut and respond as soon as possible.

BE POLITE, BUT HONEST

I get so many requests, you guys. You can't even imagine the amount of emails asking for mentorship, advice, nonprofit support, and product endorsements flooding my inbox on the regular. For years and years I agreed to every coffee date, every request to "pick my brain," and every charity opportunity that came my way, and I was drowning in it. I didn't know how to say no, because I felt a responsibility to give back and show up for others. Then I had an epiphany: every time I gave someone an hour, I was taking an hour away from my kids. Every time I gave someone an hour, that was less energy I had to devote to my marriage. Every yes to someone else was a no to me and my list of priorities. So I started being totally honest, and I did it in the most polite way possible. I told everyone who requested time that I couldn't commit to anything additionally this season because it would take time away from my family. Seriously, who is going to argue with you or be mad at you for that? Nobody. I've never once had someone push back on this, but I have had many women write back and tell me they'd never considered that perspective. A yes to their agenda is a no to yours. Be honest about what you can commit to and do it politely.

BE FIRM

This almost plays into the idea of only touching something once, because if you don't do this effectively, you'll have someone reach out again and again, which is a waste of both your time and theirs. Be firm with others in a way that doesn't leave it open-ended, unless you'd truly like to revisit the opportunity later. Also, be firm with yourself. You've made the commitment to you and your goals, and it's important that you stick to your guns. Learn to say no and to say no effectively.

PART III

SKILLS TO ACQUIRE

skill[1]

skil

noun

1. the ability to do something well; expertise.

Please note, in this section we'll be talking about skills and not talents. These are not unique and special abilities you were born with; they are learned abilities. Developing a new skill set or growing in a certain area is something accomplished with focus and time and hard work. So, good news! Even if these aren't things you currently possess in your arsenal, you're still entirely capable of making them yours. No excuses, remember? We let go of those in part 1.

SKILL 1:

PLANNING

The first time Dave and I went to Amsterdam, we got lost.

We were a young married couple, and neither of us had ever traveled to Europe before. We made all the classic mistakes: we packed too many countries into too few days, we went to every tourist location the world has ever known, we lived in fear of the "gypsies" who might steal our worldly possessions and so, though it pains me to admit it to you, we wore our passports and money under our clothes in special Velcro pouches created specifically for this purpose. Bless.

On that trip we went to London and later explored Rome and Florence and got trapped in Venice during an Italian transportation strike. But before that happened, there was Amsterdam.

I will be fully transparent. We added Amsterdam to the list because the child-nerds that we were thought it would be cool to go to a country where you could get a cup of coffee and legal marijuana at the same establishment. Did either of us smoke marijuana or even eat it inside brownies? No. Which was why it felt illicit enough to visit an entire country for just this purpose. In our defense, this was circa 2005, so marijuana wasn't easily available like it is today. Also, we were idiots. But back to Amsterdam.

We flew from London to Amsterdam on Ryanair—basically an aerodynamic cardboard box with all the luxury amenities of a medieval oubliette—but on our way in to land, the plane reared us back up into the sky. The fog was too thick, apparently, and we had to be rerouted. If you're young, you'll have to imagine a time before smartphones existed—the rest of us still have nightmares about those days, but we were in the thick of it. We were rerouted to—wait for it—an entirely different country! I honestly don't know how this is possible, but it's true. Rather than landing in Amsterdam, we landed in Frankfurt. Germany.

Y'all, I did not have a German translation book. I did not have Lonely Planet's guide to Germany with all the helpful little English phrases, because I never intended to go there. We were so stinking confused.

Somehow, through many questions and even more pantomiming, we gathered that we'd now be getting on a bus. An honest-to-goodness bus that would then drive us into Amsterdam. The bus was crammed to the gills with Europeans in giant parkas to contend with the winter temps. It smelled like my minivan after a half-full bottle has been allowed to bake inside it undetected in the Texas heat—sour and wrong. We were nauseated and not entirely positive that this was really where we were supposed to be. Next came the train. In retrospect, I'm not even sure how we made it this far. Maybe we just blindly followed the other people on the airplane/bus right onto that train, but one way or another we were finally on our way to Amsterdam. When we arrived in the city, we walked out of the train station with no clue how to get to our hotel. We had a printout of the name and the address, and we just sort of awkwardly asked one person after another.

"Do you know how to get to this hotel?" That person didn't speak English. We tried another.

"Excuse me, do you know how to get to this hotel?" Another confused person who couldn't answer us.

Person after person either didn't understand what we were asking or answered us in a language we couldn't decipher. We flagged down a taxi and showed him the address.

"Amsterdam," he told us.

"Yes! Yes, sir. Amsterdam! Can you take us?" We were exhausted and at this point had been asking people (while towing our suitcases behind us) for nearly an hour.

"Amsterdam," he said again, and when we just looked at him, confused, he drove off.

We started asking every person we passed until finally, blessedly, we found a man who spoke broken English.

"Sir, do you know how to get to this hotel?" I pointed emphatically at the address on my now wrinkled and dirty paper.

He looked at the paper, then back at us, then at the paper again. "Yes. Is Amsterdam."

"Yes, we know." I pointed to the streets around me. "Which direction? How do we get there?"

"Is Amsterdam," he said again.

I wanted to scream or cry, and he must have sensed my growing distress, because he stiltedly fought his way through his response.

"Hotel is Amsterdam," he told us. "You are here."

Horror started to dawn on me. "Where is here?" I asked him.

He shook his head. "Not Amsterdam."

You guys, we weren't even in the right city.

We were still two hours away from it. Likely we were supposed to get on another train to take us there, but we didn't know. We were sheep; we followed the crowd. What was supposed to be a two-hour flight ended up being an entire day of planes, trains, and automobiles, and we didn't get to the hotel until it was too late to do anything. I'm sure God was trying to keep me from ingesting illicit baked goods on foreign soil, but the point is still the same.

The first step toward achieving your goal is to know where you're headed. The problem is that often people think that's all they need to know. They forget one crucial piece of the puzzle: a map only works if you know both your end and your starting point. Said another way, you cannot get to where you want to go if you don't know where you are.

You need a road map. You need a starting point. You need a finish line. You need to know the guideposts and mile markers along the way. You need a plan of attack. You can talk about the things you want for your life every single day. I'm sure you can even find friends who will go to coffee with you and daydream and brainstorm, but none of that matters if you don't actually develop a real plan to get you where you want to be. People don't get lost because they're not sure where they want to go. People get lost because they start out on a path and don't keep checking to make sure they're still headed in the right direction.

How often do you set out on a road trip without a map or directions? The only time we do that is if we don't care where we end up—we just want to take a drive and listen to music and see what we find. But if we actually have somewhere we want to be, if we actually have a destination in mind, we always have a map. Why? Because a map can get us there faster and more efficiently. Because when we see something from a ten-thousand-foot view, we're able to plan for and anticipate things that might pop up along the way. It's much harder to have any kind of real strategy when you're on the road.

I have used this road-map strategy for every major work project or personal goal I've taken on over the last fifteen years. It's how I landed all my major clients in the event industry. It's how I booked press for myself without a publicist and used that exposure to propel my career. It's how I trained for a 10K, then a half marathon, and finally a full marathon. It's how I wrote my first book and got my first book deal. It's the strategy and intention behind everything in my life from products to relationships, and I'm convinced there isn't anything it couldn't work for. It's not complicated; it only has three components. The trick is to approach these elements out of the usual order we expect them to be in.

See, we're taught to start at one, then get to two, then end up at three. This is incredibly confusing if you don't know what step two is. And how are you supposed to know what the steps are if you've never taken them before?

I've found that if I flip the order and start with the finish line, then contemplate where I'm starting from, I can more easily define the steps in the middle that will take me from one place to another.

Here's how I do it:

THE FINISH LINE

First of all, you've got to start at the end. Counterintuitive, perhaps, but super effective in figuring out what direction your path should go. By now we've done enough work together that you should already have one clear and defining objective, one goal you're focused on right now. That's where you start.

To give you an idea of exactly how I've used this road-map strategy, I'm going to share a personal goal of mine from the past. I wanted to have a cookbook. I was a food blogger at the time, and having a cookbook felt like the ultimate goal! That was my finish line. I figured out my very specific *what* by zeroing in on my very specific *why*. I wanted a product for my fans that would commemorate my family recipes and be a first product offering that was in line with my brand at the time.

THE STARTING POINT

Now that you know where you want to go, you need to practice some self-awareness and be really honest about where you're starting from. What assets, resources, and habits do you currently have that are going to help you with your journey? How can you expand on them and use them for exponential growth? What habits do you have that might derail you or push you off course? How can you be intentional in planning around those in advance so they don't sneak up on you? What good habits could you develop to replace those negative ones? My starting place for my cookbook was great. As a food blogger I knew photographers and designers and a food stylist to help me make it all look incredible. What I didn't have was a literary agent or experience in the cookbook space. I was super honest with myself about what I did and didn't have access to, and then I got to work!

THE GUIDEPOSTS + MILE MARKERS

Now that you know where you're going and you know where you're starting, the next step is a brainstorm of every single thing you can think of that might help you get closer to the goal. And a great brainstorm always starts with great questions.

For instance, how could I get a cookbook deal? At the time I had no idea, so I headed over to Google (I swear to you, the answer for literally everything exists on the internet for free), and I asked that exact question. There were all kinds of answers, and I wrote down each and every one in a big idea soup—that's what I call my written brainstorm sessions, because they always look like a big messy bowl of possibility. Anytime I'm creating a soup, my goal is to find at least twenty ideas for how I'm going to get there. I put down anything I can think of, and since it's a brainstorm, I don't debate whether the idea is good. I just write it down.

Write a book proposal, get a literary agent, grow my social media following, establish myself as an expert in this field, research book proposal, hire graphic designer, hire photographer, do recipe testing, and so on.

The problem with stopping at this soup, besides the fact that it's overwhelming, is there are too many possible directions to head. We want to create a clear direction, and this brainstorm page, while awesome to get your wheels spinning, is likely to create a lot of stops and starts and unproductive attempts. So, in order to move forward, we've got to get it organized. The question is, How do we do that? The answer is, surprisingly, with another question.

Look at your brainstorm and ask yourself, of all the ideas you've got there, what are the three major things that, if you actually achieved them, they would—without question—get you to your goal? Getting from twenty ideas down to three might seem impossible, especially since so many of them would be helpful, but I'm convinced that if you force yourself to come up with only three, those three will be the guideposts you'll need to get you back on track if you get lost along the way. How do you choose your three? Go to your end goal and ask yourself, *What is the step that comes just before this?* Then choose two more guideposts working back from there.

The thing about a guidepost is that it's something you cannot easily achieve without taking a bunch of other steps to get you there. People often hesitate to write these down, because they seem nearly as impossible as the dream itself. Their brains immediately start coming up with all the reasons that it's going to be impossible to achieve. Maybe they're like, "Sure, sure, sure. I can write down the thing, but eventually reality creeps back in, and my negative self-talk creeps back in, and I don't know how I'm going to get there, and gosh, I'd like to do this thing, but I don't . . ."

No, no, no, no. Don't focus on the lack. Don't worry about *how* you'll hit each guidepost. *How* will stop you dead in your tracks. Obsessing over the how is what stops us from going anywhere. Right now we're not focused on the *how*; we're focused on the *what*. As in, what steps do I need to take to make this goal a reality?

For my publishing journey, my road map started to take form

when I forced myself to come up with my three guideposts. The very last step before getting a deal for publishing a cookbook is submitting a proposal to publishing houses: guidepost number three. Okay, so what's the step before that? Well, Google told me that in order to submit to a publishing house, I had to have a literary agent. No publisher will just blindly accept a manuscript off the street, so finding a literary agent became the second guidepost on my map. Then I asked myself what I would need to secure a literary agent. There are so many ways to land one, but they all had one central thing in common: I'd need to create a proposal of some kind to explain what I wanted to do. That became the first guidepost in my road map.

I had a starting point and an ending point and three major guideposts on the way. Now, *now* I was able to figure out the *how*, or, as I like to call them, the mile markers. I had forced myself to come up with three major guideposts, but the mile markers can be numerous because these are all the little things, all the *hows* you're going to need to figure out and do to get you to that next guidepost.

To identify them, you start at the beginning of your road map for the first time since you began laying it out, and you do another idea brainstorm with this question: What do I need to do to get from my starting point to my first guidepost? I suggest putting on some pump-up music and writing as much as you can as fast as you can, anything that pops into your head. Don't even think about it. Just write down every idea you can think of that in any way could help you get to your first guidepost. I call this a possibilities list.

Let's say your goal is to start a wedding planning business (yes, I'm writing what I know), which means that your third guidepost would be to land some clients. Well, then your second guidepost would be to make sure your potential clients know about your business: you'll need a portfolio, an Instagram account, or a website where potential brides can see your work. Of course, none of that matters if you don't have any work to show off, so your first guidepost has to be the creation of that content. Since I have made this exact possibilities list to get me to this exact guidepost, I can tell you that the questions I asked myself along the way looked like this: How do I get content? Photographers? Florists? Should I partner with someone to design and produce different looks? Could I volunteer my time with other wedding planners in exchange for photos in my portfolio? How have other people created portfolios? Are there books I could read on this topic? Are there influencers I can follow who are talking about this subject?

Whenever I'm not sure how to get to the next step, even today, I create a possibilities list and fill up pages and pages with things like, "Oh, yeah. Sarah's cousin works for that company that I've been dying to have as a client." There were many times when I didn't remember I had a connection until I sat down and made my list. This happens because we spend so much time sitting in what we don't have that we don't realize the access we actually do have.

WARNING: this is often the place where the dreamers start wandering off the side of the highway to gather wildflowers rather than making any real traction toward their destination. For example, if my first guidepost is clearly "create a book proposal," there are all sorts of things I could brainstorm to get me there: researching book proposals, creating a Pinterest board of ideas, finding out the structure of a book proposal for this genre, talking to authors in this space and asking them for advice, finding a graphic designer to help me lay it out, taking an online course to learn about book proposals, going to a writer's conference, and so forth. Most people see this list and get excited, thinking, *Holy crap, look at all these ideas!* Simultaneously they convince themselves that all ideas are created equal and all of them will be effective. Don't get it twisted! Not all of these ideas will get me anywhere closer to my goal, but many of these ideas are way sexier and way more fun than the tasks that actually will get me there.

Creating a Pinterest board? That's so fun. I think I'll do that. Oooh, and a writer's conference? I've always wanted to go to one of those. And brainstorming with my new friends from my writing club? That's perfect! We convince ourselves that all of these are great ideas and that we're spending dedicated time working toward our guidepost, when really we're just walking around in circles. If I'm being honest with myself, I know the exact step that comes right before creating a book proposal. I don't want to do it because it's the hardest, suckiest part of writing a book, but I know what it is. I've got to actually write the words.

I want to encourage you here, because if you're being realistic then you must realize that a big part of the reason you haven't achieved the guidepost already is that your mile markers, while doable, take hard work. Mile markers are the *achievable steps*, and you can take one after another to get you to the destination. But they're always work. Always.

As I sit writing this book, *Girl, Wash Your Face* has been out in the world for a handful of months. At this point it's sold 722,000 copies and become a #1 *New York Times* bestseller, and I've received thousands and thousands of notes from women all over the world telling me how helpful it's been in their lives. What a gift! What an incredible blessing that's so big I couldn't even have dreamed of it! Do you think that success makes it any easier to write *this book*? No. Writing is always hard for me. It's always work. Even though I've done it so many times before, even though I've been able to experience success with it, even though I believe so deeply in what I'm writing about—even then it's a slog to the finish line.

The idea is not that a road map will magically make the journey easier; the idea is that a road map will make the journey effective. I believe deeply in what you're capable of. I think you can achieve anything you set your mind to, but you've got to set your mind to it. You've got to be relentless in your pursuit and flexible in your methods.

So buck up, and start creating the mile markers that will get you to each guidepost. If you're not sure what they are, then ask yourself better questions. For instance, if my question is "How can I sign with a literary agent?" my answer at the time would have been "I have no idea!" Which gets me exactly nowhere. But if I change the question to, "Who might know how I can get a literary agent?" or "Where could I research to find out the answer?" or "Are there books or podcasts or YouTube videos about this?" then suddenly my answers are endless. Remember, if you're not getting effective answers, it's because you're not asking effective questions.

Also, don't get freaked out about all the possibilities. This goal of yours is going to feel like something gigantic when you begin. Remember how to eat an elephant? One bite at a time! When you're first starting to work toward a goal, it's so easy to get overwhelmed. There are so many things to do and never enough hours to do them. If you're like me, you have eighteen to-do lists going, and they've got everything on them. If it feels overwhelming, it's because you're trying to do too many things at one time. Slow down. Make a daily list. Make a weekly list. Make a monthly list. Now double-check them. Is everything on those lists essential to helping you get to the next guidepost? If not, revise and refocus.

Now you've got your road map. The next step is almost as important as figuring out the rest of it. In between you and the goal that you've always wanted are three words. Maybe you write them down on a sticky note. Girl, maybe you should get it tattooed on your body, but it's this simple: go all in.

Go all in. Take massive action immediately. Not on Monday, not at the new year, not next month, but right now, today. Take massive action on the first mile marker on your road map.

By the way, creating a road map in the first place is going to be a massive action for many of you. But please don't stop there! Stay in. For a lot of people, it's easy for them to go all in; they just don't stay there. Something will happen and life gets in the way, and they fall off the wagon and think, *Ugh, now it's all downhill.*

No. No! Sister, half the battle in between you and where you want to go is just your willingness to stand back up. Everybody falls down, everybody slips up, everybody makes mistakes, everybody gets off course. Plenty of people set out headed toward their goal—they've got their road map, they're following along—and then all of a sudden something happens. Maybe it's something simple like slipping off their diet. Maybe they miss one week of training and then it's two, and suddenly a whole month is gone. Maybe it's been six months or six years since they sat down at their computers to write. Whatever has happened, whatever you did or didn't do, shame isn't the answer to overcoming it. It's done, it's in the past, and beating yourself up about it won't change anything. Not only is that true, but so is the fact that it's not a life sentence. Anything other than death is temporary. The problem is that you're letting a short-term choice become your long-term decision. You believe that what happened in the past is who you are. That's BS.

Who you are is defined by the next decision you make, not the last one. So get planning, make your road map, and take the next step.

SKILL 2:

CONFIDENCE

Confidence matters.

Confidence is the belief that you can count on yourself—that you trust your gut in the place you find yourself in. It matters a great deal to anyone in business, particularly if your job or company requires you to promote yourself as a way to get to the next level. But it also matters a ton in your personal life and how you think about yourself and your dreams. I don't think we talk about it enough.

If you feel like a crappy mom, if you feel totally unprepared to take on your role as mom each day, how likely are you to enjoy your life and show up well for your babies?

If you've always dreamed of doing a triathlon but you believe you're terrible at any physical activity and are positive you'll never figure it out, how likely are you to successfully take on the next race?

Confidence matters, and here's the magic: confidence is a skill. It's not something you're born with. Certainly if you were raised in a particular way, then confidence might have been instilled in you from childhood, but if you weren't so lucky, please know that it's something you can develop and that you absolutely should pursue. Here are three key things I've found make a big difference for building up self-confidence:

HOW YOU LOOK

This chapter is coming at you live from one of the most highfalutin beauty parlors in the Western Hemisphere. Nine Zero One Salon on Melrose Place in Los Angeles, to be specific. As I sit here, writing feverishly on my laptop, a team of beautiful twentysomethings are working to cover up my roots and add in highlights around my face. A myriad of tiny bowls filled with different colored potions are spread out in every direction. They're painting color onto my hair with the precision of a pediatric heart surgeon, all while chatting amongst themselves about which house they're renting for Coachella and whether or not Kristin Cavallari's new diet book is any good. Their work is equal parts artistry and witchcraft, and when they finish I'll look the best I've looked since the last time I left this chair. The entire procedure costs as much as a used Sebring convertible . . . and that's just the coloring process.

I have hair extensions and eyelash extensions, and I got a boob job five years ago because I was tired of my post-breastfeeding chest resembling tube socks filled with pudding. I know not everyone approves of spending all of this time and money on your physical appearance. I know, because they send me notes. "How can you tell us to love ourselves the way we are but then spend money on makeup and hours getting your hair colored?" I understand that this might seem hypocritical to you, but you may have missed one key distinction. I do believe we should love ourselves the way we are . . . the way I am just happens to involve fake eyelashes.

In all seriousness, I love makeup. Have you ever seen those videos on YouTube where gals do different looks and use a hundred different makeups and fourteen different brushes just to shade one eyelid? That is artistry! That is a skill acquired over years of effort, and I bow down. When I put on my own makeup I think it's fun, and I like how I look afterward. I don't do it because you think I should look a certain way—or because society likes a well-contoured cheekbone—I do it because I like it.

I invest a lot of money and a lot of time into the way I look because it makes me feel—well shoot, I guess it makes me feel great, and when I feel great I feel confident.

Before I dig into this more, I've got to add some disclaimers. I'm positive that not everyone I know ties some of (or a lot of) their confidence into their looks. Some of us were raised right. Some of us had upbringings that said it's your heart and your mind and your spirit that matter—that is how it should be. But just because it should be a certain way doesn't mean it is. If I'm going to talk about what really works instead of what should work, then we've got to be truthful. Every woman I know—I cannot think of one single woman who doesn't—feels more confident when she likes the way she looks.

Every single one.

Disclaimer number two? Confidence comes from *you* liking the way you look, not from you looking any certain way.

I love big hair and eyelashes and shoes with some kind of heel. My friends, Sami and Beans? They love sneakers and hats, and I'm pretty sure they think they look worse with a lot of makeup on. It's not their preferred style. If the greatest makeup artist in the world gave them a full makeover, they would appreciate the artistry but hate the results. It would actually make them feel less confident because they wouldn't recognize themselves when they looked in the mirror. Gaining confidence from your appearance isn't about having a specific style; gaining confidence from the way you look is about having a *personal* style.

Do you love sneakers and button-downs? Are you into sleek and straight hair and minimal makeup? Is your wardrobe as bright and eclectic as your personality? Yes to all of it! Yes to any of it. Yes to knowing who and what you are and allowing it to be represented in the way you look.

I know there will be people who disagree with me. I know there will be people who read this and think I'm being superficial. I understand that it seems vapid to start a chapter on confidence and ground it in physical appearance—in how you look instead of how you feel—but I don't think the alternative would be helpful. At least it wouldn't have been helpful for me back in the day. I read so many books that told me to look inside or pray or say mantras or affirmations to make myself feel more confident. I did it for years as a way of boosting myself up. But I honestly never felt the part of a confident woman until I learned how to look the part of a confident woman. And the crazy thing is, my version of confidence probably looks nothing like yours. The point is not that you replicate someone else's ideal. The point is that you figure out your own.

I wish this were a picture book so I could show you any shot of me from basically 2003 to 2016. In fairness to the Rachel of the past, I do feel like I improved over time. But it was also slow going and vaguely tragic, and it was entirely because I didn't know how to dress for my body type or do my hair or my makeup. Not knowing how made me feel insecure, but I would never actually admit to that. Instead I loudly proclaimed that I wasn't "that kind of girl." I would swipe on a little eyeliner and some lip balm and throw my air-dried, frizzy hair in a bun, all while militantly telling myself that women who cared so much about their appearance were airheads who were focused on the wrong things.

So why was it, then, that every single time I had to get my hair and makeup done for press or TV, I felt like a hundred million dollars? How come I would plan date nights with my husband whenever I knew I was going to have makeup on from a shoot? How come I always felt better, had more energy and a better attitude, every time I felt like I looked great? Because when you like the way you look, you'll love the way you feel.

This was a big learning curve for me as a grown-up, and it all started with a boob job.

———

It's true. I did get a boob job. It's sort of a crazy thing to admit, but I'm doing it. I'm sure some of you are like, "Good for you, girl." That's everyone's dream postbaby, and some of you are like, "You're an embarrassment to feminists everywhere!" But I did it, and since I always try to be honest about the things I go through in my life, I'm telling you about it now.

I guess, let's start with why.

Hmmm . . . how do I explain this delicately? When I got pregnant the first time, I had lovely little B-cups. I loved them, and they loved me back. After the baby was born, the milk came in, and those lovely Bs became E-cups. No, that's not a typo. That's a cup size. E . . . as in Elephant . . . as in Enormous . . . as in Yowza!

So the twins went from little to big and then back again. After that round I gave birth to two more children, which means that whole E for everyone rating—it happened two more times! After my last son, Ford, was born, I started exercising more and eating better, and I maintained a healthier weight, which was awesome. But that weight meant that my boobs, which were already in a little bit of a sad state, became . . . nothing. I don't mean that they were worn out. I don't mean that they looked tired. I mean that there was nothing there, no filler, no cushion. The cup, in this case, was definitely half-empty. So where before

I'd never really thought about my breasts much, now I noticed them all the time.

I hated to wear a bathing suit. I hated to go without a bra or, even worse, topless in front of my husband. Mostly, I hated how focused I was on something so trivial. Dave never said anything. He approached them just like he always had, with reverence and the unfettered joy of a straight man seeing boobs, but my issues got worse. Honestly, I'm not one to wallow for long. I'm a fixer. And while I can't fix everything, this was something I definitely could do something about. I decided I was going to have them lifted back up.

I found a doctor who was awesome and who also has kids, so she totally got what I was looking for. I made Dave go with me to the appointment, and I asked a million questions, which mostly had to do with whether I'd die on the table like the mom from *Clueless* and whether I'd lose sensitivity (because that might almost be as bad as death). They took some pictures for my chart, which, let me tell you, is freaking abysmal! Nobody needs to see their sad little boobs through the lens of an HD camera under intense lighting.

I ended up choosing the smallest implant they make, because every time I tried on the bigger sizes, I felt uncomfortable. I didn't want to be someone new; I just wanted to feel like my old self. And, as Dave put it when I asked him what he thought, "You're beautiful no matter what you do. Just choose something that makes you feel good." Smart man.

We scheduled the appointment for surgery. I was so excited, but as the day got closer and closer, I started to freak out. Not about whether to do it, but about whether I'd live. I had three beautiful children at the time, and surgery is scary. What if something happened to me because of my own vanity? Can you imagine what a horrible legacy I'd leave behind?

"Oh, my mom was super healthy, but she wanted to look good in a tank top and now she's dead!"

I made my friends promise that, in the case of my untimely demise, they would help perpetuate the myth for my children that I'd died in a Doctors Without Borders mission. Never mind that I'm not a doctor; in this made-up past I was much more valiant than I actually am.

The morning of the surgery, I was a mess. I started freaking out as soon as I got into the room with all the pre-op stuff, and Dave had to come sit with me. It didn't help that my anesthesiologist turned out to be blond, tan, and basically a very, very young Ken doll. Like, whatever age you have to be to have just made it out of medical school, that's what we were dealing with here. His name was Dr. Aiden, he said. He'd spent the morning surfing, he said.

Surfing.

All I could think while they wheeled me to the room was, *Oh, precious Savior, this surfing child-doctor is going to see my boobs.*

Sometimes when I get nervous, I manage those nerves by talking nonstop, so I was chattering nervously when the model-doctor put the IV into my arm. That IV, though I didn't realize it at the time, was filled with some really strong drugs. I remember telling the assembled medical personnel that no anesthesiologist should look like this guy. He was supposed to be bald and sixty-plus years old . . . he should look like Danny DeVito. I remember all the nurses and doctors laughing at me, and I remember thinking, *Shut up, Rach, shut up!* but I was too far gone.

I could not shut up.

The last thing I remember saying before slipping off into oblivion was, "Please, Dr. Aiden, whatever you do, don't look at my destroyed boobs!"

Not. Even. Kidding.

And then I woke up, and . . . I lived! I was so excited to be alive that I didn't even mind that it felt like my chest had gone twelve rounds with a prizefighter. Between the anxiety and pre-op and the unexpected presence of a ridiculously good-looking anesthesiologist to make me more nervous, not to mention the recovery time, it was all quite an ordeal. But, in the end, I absolutely thought it was worth it and I still do. Will you think so too? Maybe, maybe not. I understand that not everyone will agree with my choices, but that's okay. The point was that it was something I wanted to do for myself, something I knew would make me feel more confident. I decide how I want to look, and when I made the choice to change something in such a drastic and permanent way, it made me start to consider other things I hadn't before.

Remember, for years I'd told myself that women who cared about their looks were artificial and vapid. But now I'd done possibly the most artificial thing ever: I'd had someone put the medical equivalent of a balloon inside my body in an attempt to feel more confident. And you know what? It worked.

I loved my new boobs! Five years later, and I still love them.

But now I needed to reconcile the story I'd always told myself with the new reality I was facing. I had done something purely for vanity's sake, but I didn't feel like a vain person. I didn't sit around all day obsessing over my looks, and I certainly didn't judge people for theirs. So if it was possible to still be the same woman who was so focused on personal growth—on improving what was on the inside—then could it be possible that my former beliefs about how valuable, or not valuable, our outside appearances are were founded more in my insecurities than in actual evidence?

Well, obviously.

Our own insecurities on any subject either spark our curiosity or they feed our judgment. We either see the opportunity to grow and so allow ourselves to wonder, ask questions, and do research, or we become fearful and close down the idea immediately. *Only an idiot would consider that. Only frivolous people try something new when they're already on a path.* Your insecurity makes it so that anyone who is doing it differently than you is an indictment on all the ways you're not measuring up.

Making sweeping judgments about others or—more upsetting—about yourself isn't helping you. Maybe you'll try getting a blowout or try skinny jeans or try open-toe booties with a stacked heel, and maybe you'll hate them. But you are never going to know if you aren't open to considering it. If your self-confidence is through the roof, then keep doing whatever it is you're doing now, but if you don't feel good about the way you look, what are you waiting for?

Have you decided this is just what life is like? Stop buying into that! Life is whatever you believe it is. So what if you never knew how to dress in high school or how to style your hair? That was a long time ago, and you're not that girl anymore. I know I sound like a broken record, but every single thing you want to know how to do is in a YouTube video right now for free. Curling my hair, putting on makeup, selecting the best outfits for short girls, how to wear white jeans—literally all things I've learned in the last five years. Don't believe me? Go look on my Instagram and scroll on back. It won't take you long until you're like, *Holy crap, what was she wearing? What was going on with that hair and those eyebrows?*

Go ahead. I give you full permission to creep on my old photos. Just because you used to be a certain way doesn't mean you have to stay that way. Just because you feel insecure doesn't mean you can't make a change. If you don't like the way you look, if you don't love your personal style, then figure it out! Make an investment! And don't let anyone make you feel guilty about it.

HOW YOU ACT

About ten years ago I was a successful event planner in Los Angeles, and I'd built up a name for myself in the luxury wedding space. I loved the work, but after years of bridezillas and working through every weekend of the year, I longed to grow into the corporate space, which didn't have any of the emotional baggage that wedding planning did.

As I mentioned earlier, I've always been in the habit of calling my shot, figuring out my finish line, and then creating a road map from there. In this instance, my dream client/event was the Sundance Film Festival. It was super glamorous and filled with celebrities and also took place in a really difficult setting. Producing the luxury of a Los Angeles event in a tiny mountain town in Utah that's only accessible by a canyon likely to be covered with snow this time of year? I knew if I could pull that off it would launch my company into a new stratosphere.

Sundance became my goal.

So then I backed up from there. If I wanted to get some attention for producing a great event at Sundance, then it needed to be an event that would get notice. I did some research and learned that *Entertainment Weekly* was the major player at the festival. They threw the biggest parties, had the most celebrity attendees, and therefore got the most press coverage. They were the best, and I wanted to work with the best.

I was in no way qualified to do it. Not all events are created equal, and a film festival in Utah is something else entirely. Still, there was no way I would ever actually learn how to produce the type of event I wanted to create if I didn't ever throw my hat in the ring. I went for it. I asked a friend of a friend of a friend to make an introduction, and I finally got a phone call with the events team.

I pitched my heart out.

They weren't interested. They were very kind about it, but they knew I was out of my league. Like a dog that suddenly decides to walk upright on two legs, just because you might be able to do something doesn't mean it's the right choice. They weren't even interested in having me bid for the job.

I was discouraged, but discouragement won't get you anywhere. Every other week—for the next eighteen months—I followed up with my contact at *Entertainment Weekly*. I sent her party inspiration and details on new drinks. I told her the best DJs to hire and cute outfits the staff could wear. I intentionally added value wherever I could and never one time asked if they'd consider me for a job.

One day, the *EW* events person called out of the blue. "We need a caterer for Sundance. You do that, right?"

I absolutely did not own a catering company, but I had worked so hard to get this opportunity to partner with them that I jumped at the chance. "Of course! What do you need?"

This moment bidding my first Sundance job is always the best example I have to give when someone asks me about the idea of "fake it 'til you make it." I hate that phrase, because it implies you've got nothing else to back it up. There's a big difference between faking something that you have no idea how to do and having the confidence to step into a role that you don't have full training for yet.

There's a study that shows that when a man is considering a new job, he will apply for a position he feels he's at least 60 percent qualified for. His confidence tells him that he'll make up the other 40 percent by learning as he goes. By contrast, that same study shows that the average woman feels that she must be 100 percent qualified to apply for anything.[1] Okay, think about this for a second. How on earth can you be qualified for something you've never done? It's a catch-22. You won't put yourself out there. You never try for fear of failure, so you never grow to the next level.

When it came to the Sundance opportunity, I absolutely wasn't a caterer, but I had worked with and managed caterers as vendors for years, and I knew what would be involved. I had connections and resources and enough skill with research and planning to get myself the rest of the way there. I wasn't faking it, because it never occurred to me that I wouldn't be able to figure it out if I needed to. I had years of practice to back me up—certainly nothing at that level, but I was confident that I hadn't ever let a client down and I certainly wasn't about to start. I would *never* take money from someone for a service I didn't have the ability to provide. But I also would never have been able to grow my skill set if I hadn't continuously pushed myself to the very edge of it.

That single Sundance event launched my business into an entirely new level, just as I had believed it might. I turned that first year as a caterer into the next year as an event planner. Soon we were producing lounges and events for every studio and brand that wanted to celebrate in Park City. Sundance became my most profitable contract. In fact, it's what paid for the start of The Chic Site and hiring staff when I finally decided to transition into this space.

So many good things came out of a willingness to act confident even when I didn't always feel confident. It's like anything else. You can make yourself feel anything you set your mind to as long as you back it up with action. I acted confident in what I could do as an event planner, and then I backed it up with research and hard work to arm myself with the skills necessary to pull it off.

WHO YOU HANG OUT WITH

I know I've already touched on this a bit with the whole "you become the five people you hang out with most" topic, but it bears repeating here. Years ago my sister had graduated from cosmetology school and was unsure where to go from there. She liked the idea of working in the beauty industry in some capacity, but she wasn't confident about building up a client roster in this new industry—a must for any hairstylist. She tried several different assistant jobs at salons, and while she liked interacting with the people, she was still struggling to find her footing.

As fate would have it, an acquaintance of mine sent out an email with a job description she was looking to fill. The acquaintance owned a spa, and they needed a manager. They'd tried several different people in the role, but nobody seemed to be a good fit. I read through the description, and with every passing line item I got more and more excited. I immediately forwarded it to Mel.

"You should totally apply for this job!" I scream-texted her.

She still wasn't sold on the job she was then working in the salon, so she went ahead and pursued—and subsequently landed—this role as a spa manager.

She was so nervous that first week about how it would all work out. She was new to LA and still learning to navigate the traffic and fast pace, and like most LA newbies she was a bit intimidated that she wouldn't dress right or speak correctly in this fancy spa near Beverly Hills.

A few weeks into her time there, I received an email from my acquaintance thanking me profusely for sending Melody her way. She could not stop singing her praises as an exceptional employee. This didn't surprise me at all. I knew that my sister was smart and gracious, and I knew she was an incredibly hard worker. What was surprising is what happened about six months later.

Melody became a totally different woman.

She was calm and poised and totally confident in herself and her skills. She wasn't anxious anymore about her new city or her new role or what she would do next. She wasn't afraid to give her opinion, and she didn't worry about what people thought.

I remember saying to Dave, "Have you noticed how great Mel is doing? I wonder what caused such a big shift?"

A few weeks later I went to the spa she worked at to get a facial, and it hit me. Melody went from being at a school filled with young people who were unsure about where they were going or how they'd make a career to working for a successful business filled with—wait for it—confident women. All day long she interacted with coworkers who were at the height of their professions—they had to be to work at a place like this. All day long she helped clients who were successful in life and in business—they had to be to afford a place like this. Without even trying to or being aware of it, she'd absorbed their confidence like osmosis.

You want to be more confident? Hang out with people who are.

I know that confidence isn't often described as a learned behavior, but I truly believe it's a skill you can learn like any other. Be mindful of the people you hang out with, the words you use, and the way you present yourself to the world around you. Pay attention to the times or the circumstances that make you feel the most self-assured, and then work to cultivate more opportunities like those. This shift in perception, particularly for any of you who are in business, can truly be life changing.

SKILL 3:

PERSISTENCE

I've heard a lot of people say things like "a goal is a dream with a deadline." Or "you've got to give yourself a timeline." I struggle with that idea because none of the success I've experienced in my personal life has been quick. If I had given myself a timeline of a year or even two, I would have given up a long time ago. It took me two years to grow enough of a social media following that a literary agent would take me seriously enough to consider my book proposal. It took another six months after that to submit the proposal to publishing houses to see if an editor would take a chance on a cookbook deal. It was eighteen more months before that book hit the market. So much work was necessary just to get to that place.

I posted a couple of pictures on Instagram recently. The first picture was from my very first TV segment for the local morning news. I had pitched for months and finally gotten booked for a segment on National Junk Food Day, wherein the KTLA morning news team and I tried out the weirdest junk food on the market at that point. Think deep-fried Oreos and pickles brined in cherry Kool-Aid. Peabody material it was not. The second picture I shared was from my very first time on the *Today Show*. In it I'm the filling in a Hoda and Kathie Lee sandwich, and I'm smiling so big and brightly that my face is about to crack in half. I was ecstatic that day because I had always, always wanted to be booked for a segment on the *Today Show*. What I need to point out—besides the fact that my hair looked so much better after I started going to a real colorist instead of using dye from a box—is that the first picture is from 2010 and the second photo is from 2018.

Eight years, you guys. It took me eight years to achieve that goal, and the road was long and hard. It started with that first junk-food segment, and after that I begged, borrowed, and stole to land more opportunities. I would snag a Fourth of July BBQ segment here or a Thanksgiving Day segment there. At the time I was flying solo at work, which meant that every single time I convinced someone to have me on their show, I had to find a way to make it work with no money and no help. I could only "buy" props that I could easily hide the price tag for so I could return them after the show. I would buy, haul, design, set, straighten, and clean up all by myself. I changed from set-up clothes to on-air clothes in gross bathroom stalls or in the back seat of my car (local news shows don't tend to have the nicest accommodations). Usually by that point I would have sweat off all my makeup and my hair would be a frizzy mess. I wasn't cute, but my table was, and I was always prepared to give the funniest, most informative segment they'd ever seen on everything from Saint Patrick's to Arbor Day.

Going after that kind of press all by myself sucked, but I didn't have the money for a publicist or a designer or even an assistant to help me set it up. What I did know was my goal, and I understood that hard work was the only leverage I had. When I got my first chance to do a national show, I jumped at it, even though it was on a topic I didn't know and had to research long and hard just to be able to talk about it intelligently for six minutes. For years I built relationships with TV producers. I pitched hundreds of segments that got rejected for every one that got accepted. I became known as a pinch hitter; I was the person who would jump on a plane last minute and cover if someone else got sick. If you needed an "expert" to show up and talk about literally anything, I was your girl. I worked my butt off—and it still took eight years.

It took me six books and five years to finally get a bestseller. It took me eight years to get on the *Today Show*. It took me four years and thousands of photos on Instagram to get one hundred thousand followers. I could keep listing things out for you one after another of how long it has all taken to get from there to here, but the point is this: it never went as fast as I wanted it to, and if I had given up because I hadn't achieved my goal by a certain date, I wouldn't have achieved any of the things you know me for today.

For all my dreamers, for all my hustlers, for all my girls reading this who are building and planning, don't you dare compare your beginning with someone else's middle! Don't you dare listen when someone tells you that you need to have an end date. Your mile markers—remember, those are the things you *can* control—those should have dates attached so that you're being productive and efficient. But your guideposts? Those are more nebulous and harder to achieve, and you may have to come at them six ways before you find something that will help you break through.

It's easy to see someone else's success and be discouraged by it, because we assume our first efforts won't measure up. Of course they won't! None of my success has been a meteoric rise. What you see now is over a decade of hard work and focus and standing back up every time I got knocked down. You don't have connections? Or money? Or access? I didn't either! I had work ethic and a dream and the patience and perseverance to see it through.

It's going to be a journey and you're going to have to fight to get where you want to go, but it's also going to be worth it.

One of my favorite signs I ever saw during a half marathon was a poster that read, "If it was easy, everyone would do it!" I love the reminder that achieving a goal is hard, but I'm still here. So are you. The reason that we're willing to stay on the road, to keep pushing to get to the next level, is that *we're not like everyone else*. It's not easy to achieve a goal. It's tough—but, girl, so are you!

The reason people give up or fall off or aren't willing to keep moving forward is because they believe this goal that they're chasing is temporary. This is something that we have been sold by media for most of our lives. "Try this, now try that, now do this diet, now try this exercise, now do this thing, now keep switching, now keep changing." This type of behavior isn't effective in the pursuit of an achievement. This type of behavior is only effective as a means of confusion. Because here's the deal . . . if brands and media and the news can confuse you, they can sell you more stuff.

Think about it. Fifty years ago, the only way to lose weight was simple: burn off more calories than you consume. It's a simple solution that works. Is it easy? No way. The waffle fries at Chick-fil-A are delicious and way more fun to eat than broccoli. But the diet industry wouldn't exist if the answer was simple and straightforward. So, instead, we've been bombarded with a million different answers, all of which are confusing. Should you go Paleo or Whole30 or Atkins or South Beach or vegan or gluten-free? Each season there is something new and different to try, and every single one of them is attached to something you can buy: books, powders, frozen meals, plans, programs, pills, etc., all to answer the confusion you feel about diet and weight loss.

This is only one industry, you guys. This attitude of flitting from one possible solution to another like a drunk butterfly shows up in every single kind of consumer good. Is it any wonder that you're trying to achieve your answer, your goal, by trying something for a little while, then giving up when it doesn't work and trying something else? Is it any wonder you're not making the headway you want to make?

No. You believe this goal in your life is *temporary*. You believe it's something to be pulled on and off like your favorite hoodie. There when you want it and tucked away in the closet when you don't.

This goal, this mission of yours, this dream, this place that you're headed—this is not a temporary thing. This is not something that you're going to do for this month, or this season, or just this year. Really, truly chasing down a goal changes not just that specific aspect of your life but how you approach life on the whole. Forever.

If you're saving money to buy a house, that will require a total change in the way you spend and save. If you want to have a strong, outstanding marriage, that means rooting out any misconceptions you have about relationships and intentionally pursuing it every day. No matter what it is you're chasing down, you'll only catch it if you go all in.

This is not just a thing you do.

This is who you are now.

Forever and ever, amen.

This is not training just for this month or a season. Think about it, every professional athlete, every Olympian—Tom Brady or Serena Williams or Messi—they're training just as hard today as they were when they started. In fact, I'd argue that to operate at the level of excellence they're at today, they're training harder than ever before. The training never stops.

Because after you achieve this goal you're going to choose the next and the next and the one after that. You pursuing the best version of you, whatever this looks like, will permeate every area of your life. So stop thinking so small. Stop thinking about this with such a limited perspective, assuming what you're doing is only about what's in front of you *now*. Dig in, work hard, be patient; the time will pass by no matter what. You may as well spend it in pursuit of something more, no matter how long it takes you to get there.

SKILL 4:

EFFECTIVENESS

When I'm on deadline for a book, like right now, I spend huge chunks of my typical workday away from my team so I can work without being disturbed. On this particular day I'm sitting at one of those long communal wooden tables that seem to be required furniture in any respectable hipster eatery. I like sitting at the communal table because I can always find someone to watch my stuff while I go to the bathroom for the eighty-seventh time this hour. The only drawback is the constant stream of people who come and go from the chairs around me, making the energy shift and change with each new addition.

The first girl who sat down today was here to work on homework. I know this because her textbook was open and she had a worksheet in front of her. She tackled it like this. She read a little bit from the book, then she looked at her Instagram for a while, then she took a picture of her coffee and her homework and posted it on Instagram—it took her another half hour to find just the right filter on VSCO. After that she focused in on the work again. She was doodling in the margin a second later. Then it was more scrolling, and some Googling, and a while later she packed up to go. Not one single thing filled out on the worksheet she came to do.

The next person who sat beside me was a bro. He was here with another bro. I actually like these kinds of dudes a lot. They're in their late twenties, full of energy and enthusiasm, and they quote Gary Vee like it's gospel. I get it. I'm in. Gary Vaynerchuk is my preacher too. In a nerdy sort of way, I was happy they were beside me. They had fancy laptops and yellow notepads, and they were brainstorming and ready to begin their work. After their initial chat they proceeded to spend two hours—I swear on my unsweetened chai tea—scrolling Instagram as well. The irony that was fully lost on them was that they were scrolling their favorite entrepreneurial feeds, showing each other quotes about perseverance and hustle, all the while oblivious to the time they were wasting.

I always feel so bad when I observe this happening to the dreamers around me. It's too easy to fall into time-wasters and busywork that get you nowhere closer to your goal. I used to do this all the time when I was a young author.

Back then, I had a really bad habit of rereading what I had written over and over and over. I would sit down to "write" for an hour and spend forty-five minutes reading what I'd already written and inevitably editing as I went along. For months I couldn't figure out why I wasn't making any real, tangible progress toward getting to my final word count. I wasn't getting anywhere because I wasn't actually doing any new work. I was just like the bros sitting next to me at the coffee shop. My guess is they'll have all sorts of collab sessions like the one they had today and finally give up on the idea they're pursuing because it's not getting anywhere. If they're anything like I was, they won't even realize that it's not the idea's fault that nothing happened. It's their own.

Have you ever worked on a goal, putting in all kinds of hours, and not made any tangible progress? My guess is it was because you didn't understand what to focus on. You thought what you needed was the time to pursue your dream, when really what you needed was to use the time you do have in an impactful way. To help you not fall into the trap of distraction disguised as productivity, here's every single thing I can think of that I've taught myself over the last decade to be not just productive but highly productive!

1. REPLACE YOUR TO-DO LIST WITH A RESULTS LIST

Remember in the last chapter when I talked about creating your road map? I mean, of course you do, that was like five minutes ago. But on the off chance you're like Drew Barrymore in *50 First Dates* and your memory is faulty, I'll remind you that your road map to your goal includes mile markers along the way. These are the stepping stones that you use to keep you focused in the direction you're headed. In order to work effectively, you need to always be working toward your next mile marker. The problem is, like those guys at the coffee shop or me in my early days of writing, it can often feel like you're working toward your next mile marker when really you're just making wider and wider circles around your current location. So, to counteract this tendency, when you sit down to work from now until forever, I want you to stop making to-do lists.

The average woman's to-do list is approximately 319 items long, which means you're never going to get through it anyway. Also, if you're anything like me back in the day, you'll spend your entire work time doing the easiest items on your to-do list, simply so you can have some items crossed out. But since none of those items get you anywhere closer to your next mile marker, it's all a big waste of time. So, let's let go of the idea of a to-do list and focus instead on creating a results list. And by "result," I mean, what is the end result I'm looking for from this work session?

A to-do list might have a line item that says "work on manuscript," but that's so nebulous. That could mean anything, and if you're already struggling to be productive, your brain will seize on any excuse to mark something as complete. So, if I daydream about a title for this book, is that working on the manuscript? If I rewrite a paragraph four times, is that working on the manuscript? If I go to drinks with a fellow author and we discuss plot points, is that working on the manuscript? No. None of it counts as working on the manuscript when what I really need is to get closer to turning in this book on time.

Right now the only thing that matters is word count. Right now I need to spend every waking minute building one sentence on top of another in order to turn this in on time. So, on my results list I will list: write 2,500 words. That's the result I want. There's no way to *sort of* write 2,500 words. You either do it or you don't. And PS, for all my fellow writers who dream of having a completed nonfiction manuscript, having a mile marker of "write 2,500 words" twenty-six times would get you there.

Let's say you've decided to set and achieve a new target for your direct sales organization. Your to-do list could have "hit new sales target" on it, but that's so open-ended. I mean, how in the world is that any direction or focus for your brain? If I talk to three new prospective clients, does that count? If I spend an hour researching how to grow in a sales organization, is that good enough? Maybe, if you're just trying to stay up-to-date in your industry, but if you want to get something you've never had, you've got to do things you've never done. Your results list should be specific: "reach out to one hundred new prospective clients every day" or "close four new contracts every week" or "increase the average sale per existing customer by 3 percent to raise overall revenue numbers."

Notice with that last one it's very focused. I like results that are specific and about more than the goal, that are also about expanding on ways to achieve the same outcome. If the last time I tried to increase my business I focused only on locking in new customers and it was difficult, I can step back and ask myself if there's a smarter way to achieve the same outcome. For instance, I could look at doing more with the clients I do have. Could I send out more emails? Can I create a process to make it easier to sell? Can I be more intentional about upselling to increase overall revenue without having to add a new client base? In this instance my goal is actually increased revenue, but I've gotten so bogged down in my to-do list that I haven't stopped to consider it in a different light. If I don't write down the result that I'm looking for first, my brain can't help me ask the right questions to get me closer to my actual goal.

So make a results list, not a to-do list. That daily results list should never be longer than five bullet points. In fact, my daily results list is typically only two or three points long at most. Because the items I'm writing down are major moves for me, when I'm able to knock out even one of them I feel ecstatic. If you overwhelm your list you're going to end every single working period feeling like you didn't accomplish much when, in reality, if you've completed at least one ideal result that pushes you closer to the next mile marker, you are wildly accomplished. That feeling of wild accomplishment needs to be your new habit. You need to make it your goal during every single working period. Not that you set aside time to work, but that you worked to accomplish the right things.

2. REEVALUATE EFFICIENCY

Knowing the right result to aim for is honestly half the battle. If you started working toward completing one ideal result for every working period and you did it consistently for the next three weeks, I think you'd be shocked to see how much progress you made. But there's something you can do to push this a little further, a little faster. Frankly, I don't know anyone working their way toward a goal who wouldn't love to get there ahead of schedule. So once you've got a clear mile marker in your future and you know the best results to aim for to get closer to it, the next question you want to ask yourself is, *Is there something I could be doing that would make this more efficient?*

If you want to dive into this question in detail, I highly recommend the book *The One Thing* by Gary Keller. In it, Keller asks a profound question. Not profound in its complexity but profound in the sense that most of us are often so busy working *inside* our goals that we never take the time to work *on* our goals. The question is basically, What's the one thing you could do right now, today, that would make everything else unnecessary?[1] When it comes to your results list, the question should be, What's the one thing I could do right now, today, that would help me achieve all of this faster, easier, more efficiently?

For instance, let's go back to my ideal result of hitting 2,500 words. I asked myself how I could get to my daily word count more efficiently, with less hassle, quicker. The answer was pretty simple and incredibly easy to implement, but if I hadn't asked the question, I absolutely wouldn't have considered it. For me, it's about writing at a coffeehouse. What's so special about a coffeehouse? Well, I have a great office with a nice desk and a good chair and access to snacks and water and bathrooms at no additional charge, and I've been writing this book for weeks during my regular office hours. But you know what else is in that office? Fourteen employees who are working on various projects that I always get pulled into. Now, just so we're clear, they're not the ones pulling me into the projects. In fact, they don't bother me at all because they know I'm on deadline. But writing is a hard and lonely slog. No matter how many times I do it, it always sucks, and when I'm at work and feeling lonely or tired of writing a paragraph, I wander out to use the restroom and along the way I find three things to stick my nose into rather than heading back to work. So 2,500 words, which should never take me more than three hours, ends up taking the better part of the day.

I was still achieving my end result, so I wasn't keen on challenging anything, but I had to ask myself, *Is there a better way to do this?* For me, that means working away from my staff. I like coffeehouses better than working from home because there's always great energy from fellow hustlers and creators and sometimes I even get ideas for chapters (like the start of this one). Working on this book at a coffeehouse means that I'm plowing through this manuscript, doing way more than 2,500 words at a time, and getting there faster than I was. If you don't ask yourself, if you don't challenge what is and isn't working, then you'll never know.

3. CREATE YOUR OWN PRODUCTIVE ENVIRONMENT

Years ago, someone I admired asked me if I could advise him on the writing process. This person was an extremely talented and sought-after speaker, but he had never written a book. I thought we'd get into word counts or plot points or how to craft an outline, but he really only wanted to know one thing: How do you create a writing retreat in your home to create the perfect atmosphere for writing?

"You don't," I told him. "You write wherever, whenever, *however* you can. Creating the perfect office won't actually help you in any way."

He didn't like my answer. He was adamant that if he could only set up the ideal space, then the process that had proven so hard in the past would become easier. I knew right then he'd never finish a manuscript. That sounds super harsh and catty, but it's the truth. This is based on my years of getting hundreds of questions just like this one. A writing room is dreamy and a luxury I hope to achieve one day. But it doesn't help you write. That's like thinking an expensive treadmill will motivate you to run. No outside factor is going to make you more productive, and if you need a certain atmosphere to be at your best, you're not truly in control of yourself.

I'm writing this sentence right now in the center seat on a packed flight. A last-minute speaking gig across the country means all the fancy seats on the plane were booked, but even though it's uncomfortable, I can't miss out on valuable writing time. Early in the morning, late at night, while my kids play in front of me at the park or at soccer practice, I write whenever, however I can. Is one space—like that hipster coffee shop or a mansion overlooking the water—more preferable? Certainly. But life doesn't work like that. If I waited for the perfect space or opportunity to be productive, I wouldn't ever have completed even one of my books. The key is to create an environment that can get you into the zone wherever you happen to be. For me, it's different kinds of playlists, or a certain song played on repeat over and over and over like white noise, that helps me focus and get into production mode, even in the most hectic of places. For you it could be a certain smell, a certain type of gum you chew (no, this is not crazy), the same exact coffee order at Starbucks—any kind of repetitious cue you can give to your brain that it's time to focus. My personal favorite zone maker is an espresso con panna and the song "Humble" as loud as my air pods will allow. In fact, it may scandalize my conservative readers to know that most of *Girl, Wash Your Face* was written to Kendrick Lamar on repeat, but, hey, when you find out what helps you get into the zone, you capitalize on it as much as you can.

4. KNOW WHAT DISTRACTS YOU AND AVOID THAT THING

Man, this sounds obvious when you write it out, but people who struggle to be or stay productive are usually too distracted to know they're distracted. Every time your focus and your energy wander, it takes a long time to get them back—if you even get them back at all. Pay attention to what steals your attention. For me, it's usually access to WiFi on my computer and the ability to see or hear the home screen of my phone. In my mind every text is urgent and possibly an employee telling me the office is burning down, every incoming email might be from Oprah, and a quick Google search to research something I'm writing about turns into a vortex rabbit hole and suddenly I find myself taking a BuzzFeed quiz to see who my ideal Disney prince might be. So guess what has to happen when I'm trying to hit a certain word count? I have to shut off my WiFi, flip my phone over, and turn the sound off so I don't see or hear any incoming messages.

5. COURSE CORRECT

It's easy to get sidetracked, and it's even easier to be moving so quickly in a direction that you don't realize it's the wrong direction. I recommend a check-in with yourself every Sunday. Sunday is the easiest time for me because it's when I plan out my week. I take the time to focus in on the outcome I want for the week and then ask myself if I'm really, truly headed in the direction of the next mile marker. If so, great! If not, what can I do this week to ensure that I get the results I'm looking for?

When it comes to efficiency, the bottom line is this: You're already doing the work. You're already putting in the time, and it would be such a waste if you were depleting your energy for no reason, or worse, potentially giving up on a great idea simply because you haven't figured out how to make greater strides toward your goal. Do an efficiency audit and figure out where you need to tighten up and shift your focus.

SKILL 5:

POSITIVITY

I once lived through fifty-two hours of labor. Fifty-freaking-two hours. I will never let my firstborn forget about this as long as I live. In fact, even after I'm gone I'm planning to arrange it so someone sends him an occasional reminder of this fact, like those men who pay a florist to deliver flowers every year on their wife's birthday after they're dead.

Anyway, it was the worst. It was so hard and exhausting and painful, and the nurses only let me have popsicles or Jell-O or chicken broth during the labor. It took forever to get to the time to push. Anyone who has lived through a similar experience will vouch for me. You wait and wait and wait, and just when it seems like you'll probably just stay pregnant forever, they announce that it's time to push. Time. To. Push.

For me, the time to push came so much later than anticipated that the epidural had started to wear off. Yes, epidural. You didn't think I went through two days of labor without drugs, did you? No. I am not that heroic. I utilized the anesthesiologist who, just so we're clear, did look like Danny DeVito—as they should—and all the good drugs they wanted to offer to me, but by go-time the pain was creeping back in. The nurses asked me if I wanted another dose, but I had read all kinds of horror stories about women who couldn't push because the meds were too strong, and I didn't want anything to slow us down further. So, like a true and proper martyr, I bravely told them I would push Jackson out without drugs.

Almost immediately I knew I had made a grave, grave mistake.

The pain was bad enough just lying there, but when I actually tried to push for the first time, it felt like Satan had stuck a flaming pitchfork right up inside me and then given it a quarter turn to the right.

"JK," I told everyone in the room. "I do in fact want those drugs just as fast as the IVs can carry them to my spinal column!"

The nurse pressed a button, the staff made some calls, they whispered amongst themselves, and then they looked at me with sad eyes. "We're so sorry. Both of our anesthesiologists are in C-sections. There's no one available to administer another dose."

What? No more drugs? No more numbing? Just me and Satan's pitchfork? My heart broke right along with my perineum.

I was in so much pain and I was so exhausted that I felt kind of delusional. I had no control over what was happening to me and had no way to escape it. It felt like no matter how many times I pushed, Jackson wouldn't come out. His heart rate began to drop, and the doctor started talking about there being too much stress on him and how maybe we'd have to do a C-section. Oddly, in the midst of utter panic, I had the greatest moment of clarity of my life. I knew I had to get Jackson out safely and calmly, and in order to do that I had to find a way to rise above the pain. I went from crying and freaking out to silent and focused. I didn't speak to Dave or my mom or the nurses or the doctors. I don't think I made another sound or even looked in anyone's direction. I was deeply inside my head, caught somewhere between fervent prayer and an internal motivational speech to my unborn child.

When Jackson Cage Hollis came screaming into the world an hour later, I don't know which of us was more exhausted. I do know that all the pain I'd been riding above came rushing back in a tidal wave so intense I still can't believe I managed to ignore it for so long. It's one of the greatest reminders I have in my life that you can choose your attitude, your focus, and your intentions for any situation, no matter what it is. That choice is often the difference between joy and suffering.

You can drink the water and wake up early and have a plan and work on it every day, but if you don't have the right attitude, you're dead in the water. All right, fine, maybe "dead in the water" is a little dramatic, but I get pretty dramatic about mindset and attitude and reaching for positivity, because it matters so dang much.

When my children are acting insane and the house is trashed and I'm seriously contemplating running away with the circus or drinking an entire box of wine, forcing myself to have a positive attitude is what saves me.

When my book is due—like right now, this book was due yesterday and yet here I am, still writing it—and work is overwhelming and my travel schedule is bananas, choosing to find the positive in every bit of it is how I stay happy.

Happy, not just sane. Not just okay. Not just getting by. But happy. I am happy and appreciative and feeling blessed 90 percent of the time, and that's not because my life is unfolding in a way that makes that easy. I am one of the happiest gals you know because I choose it every single day. I choose to practice gratitude; I choose to surround myself with things and people who support positivity. I regulate my thoughts because thoughts control feelings.

The words and phrases we use with ourselves become the soundtrack playing in the background of every moment of our lives, and there's not a single thought—good or bad—that you don't allow to be there. Are you actively monitoring that? Are you working to control the way you think about yourself and speak to yourself? Because you are not stupid, so stop telling yourself that you are. You are not ugly, so stop thinking it—even occasionally—when you look in the mirror. You are not a bitch, even if you've done bitchy things in the past. You are not ignorant or mean or unlovable or unworthy or falling short or any of the other stupid crap running through your mind.

You have to choose to be positive, to see possibility, and to see the blessings in your life each day. You choose your thoughts, and there isn't one thing running through your mind that you don't allow to be there. So every time you find yourself thinking something negative, remember DMX. Stop yourself, drop the hateful litany, shut 'em down, then replace them with good stuff. The hope is that whether you are in a season of ease or a season of hardship, you'll recognize that you're still in control of how you perceive it.

Because this is real life, not a fairy tale, and I don't for one second think it's going to be easy every day, no matter who you are or where you live. Real life is going to suck sometimes, and you'll have whole seasons that rob you of the energy you need to pursue your goal. But you still have hopes and dreams and goals for yourself and your life, and they are possible. Sometimes you're going to sprint at them headlong and sometimes you're going to take the smallest inch forward, but you've got to keep yourself in the game. You cannot control the circumstances of your life; you can only control your reaction to them.

SKILL 6:

LEAD-HER-SHIP

In sixth grade I took a picture inside a teepee. It was Girl Scout Camp circa 1995, and I still have the photo in an album covered with peace-sign stickers and multiple artistic renderings of the Stüssy *S*. In the photo I'm dressed as a young Native American girl, as imagined by a young—and ignorant—white girl. Brown tie-dye and knockoff Timberlands aren't a part of any tribal dress that I'm familiar with, but my twelve-year-old self felt beyond cool to sit beneath that mock teepee for a solo picture donated by the local Olan Mills.

Cultural appropriation aside, that particular Girl Scout experience sticks out in my mind for two reasons. One, because we made scrambled eggs by boiling them inside Ziploc bags. Since I have never been a camper, these sorts of wilderness skills still seem highly impressive. And, two, my best friend, Amanda, and I made up an entire dance routine to a Tim McGraw song and taught it to the whole squad. The song was "Indian Outlaw" (I mean, obviously), and it involved choreographed steps and moving into more than one formation. The dance was originally something we did during a break as a way to fight boredom, but it was—I'm hypothesizing here—so adorable to the assembled group of troop leaders (who were likely all a little bit in love with

Tim and that creepy pencil handlebar mustache he was rocking back then) that we were asked to perform it at campfire.

Campfire, you guys!

Campfire is the Girl Scout equivalent of the big show. It's where everything goes down. It's where patches are given out and troops are recognized; it's where we join hands in one big circle and sing, "Make new friends, but keep the old . . ." Anyone? Anyway, it's a big dang deal, and Troop 723 was about to make our campfire debut!

When the big moment came, we all danced our hearts out. And during the grand finale when the song cuts to the unexpected inclusion of "Indian Reservation" by Paul Revere and the Raiders, well, sisters, it was as if the spirit of Juliette Gordon Low herself was inside each of us!

I was a leader even then, and likely so were most of you. As little girls, many of us were the ones who organized exactly how the Barbie accessories would be distributed fairly. We were the ones who instigated playdates or ran for drama club president. It wasn't a conscious thought, but the ability to gather groups and unite them around a theme or idea was just part of us. If you're lucky, your parents encouraged you in these natural leadership skills. If you're not as lucky, they may have unintentionally tried to snuff it out. "Don't be bossy," they'd say. "You're not in charge of everyone," they'd remind you. Never mind that when one of the boys displayed these same exact characteristics it was seen as admirable. "Look at that natural-born leader," they'd comment wistfully.

Leadership isn't a trait that was encouraged in girls when I was growing up, and maybe that's why so many of us struggle with the mantle now. We don't tend to think of ourselves as leaders because that's most often reserved for business settings. I'm here to tell you I don't care who you are or what you do during the day. Working or moming or school or whatever, it's all the same to me in this area. I need you to embrace the idea that you are a leader. In fact, we all need you to do that.

I've spent the last half decade of my life building up a community of women—both online and in person—who believe in a similar philosophy as I do. We welcome and support one another regardless of what we have in common and despite our differences. We give one another space to belong and the encouragement to pursue our dreams, and I am so blessed that so many of you share my vision. I'm doubled over by how many women follow me online or come to my conference or buy my books, but here is the truth from the very bottom of my heart: I'm not looking for one more fan. I don't need one more woman to like my Instagram feed or think my shoes are cute. I'm not trying to develop a community of fans. I'm trying to develop a community of leaders.

Are you an influencer? Are you in media? Do you run a conference? A business? A podcast? Are you a mom in the PTA? Are you a teller at the local bank? Are you a volunteer for Sunday school at church? Are you a high school student? Are you a grandma of seven? Great! I need you. We need you!

We need you to live into your purpose. We need you to create and inspire and build and dream. We need you to blaze a trail and then turn around and light the way with your magic so other women can follow behind you. We need you to believe in the idea that every kind of woman deserves a chance to be who she was meant to be, and she may never realize it if you—yes, you—don't speak that truth into her life.

You'll be able to do that if you first practice the idea of being made for more in your own life. After all, if you don't see it, how do you know you can be it? If women in your community or your network marketing group or your Zumba class don't ever see an example of a confident woman, how will they find the courage to be confident? If our daughters don't see a daily practice of us feeling not only comfortable but truly fulfilled by the choice to be utterly ourselves, how will they learn that behavior?

Pursuing your goals for yourself is so important, and I'd argue that it's an essential factor in living a happy and fulfilled existence—but it's not enough simply to give you permission to make your dream manifest. I want to challenge you to love the pursuit and openly celebrate who you become along the journey. When your light shines brighter, others won't be harmed by the glare; they'll be encouraged to become a more luminescent version of themselves. That's what leadership looks like. Leaders are encouraging. Leaders share information. Leaders hold up a light to show you the way. Leaders hold your hand when it gets hard. True leaders are just as excited for your success as they are for their own, because they know that when one of us does well, all of us come up. When one of us succeeds, all of us succeed.

You'll be able to lead other women to that place if you truly believe that every woman is worthy and called to something sacred. That requires opening your eyes and your heart to certain women you may not have noticed before.

And though it may seem slightly off topic for a book on personal growth, I want to ask you to consider who you're including in your sphere of leadership. I want to challenge you to do something.

Look around you. Look at your Instagram feed. Look at the speaker lineup for your conference. Look at your staff. Look at your friends. Do they all look the same? And just so we're clear, I don't mean, do they have different hair colors or personal styles? I mean, well, frankly, I mean, are they all the exact same color? Are they all the exact same type? Do they all go to the same church? Do they all live in the same area?

I see this everywhere in female-focused media right now. I see it manifest on stages. I see it show up in the company's staff photo. I see it with the speaker lineup. I see it in the advertising. And every single time I see it I wonder, *Why isn't this homogeny upsetting to this group? Why doesn't this disparity bother them? How can they pull together sixteen speakers, only one of which is female?* Or, at a women's conference, *How can you choose ten female speakers to represent all women, and nine of them are white?* I don't think it's a conscious choice for most companies or conferences or friend circles to shun diversity. I just think that we tend to choose what we know, and what we know best are people who look and act and think like us.

But, friends, this is not what the world looks like. This is not what business or the market looks like. This is not what our community looks like.

Representation matters. It matters that you sit in an audience and see yourself onstage. It matters that a company who sells to a multiethnic, multicultural world works to bring every voice in so that they consider as many perspectives as possible. Black, white, Latino, Asian, old, young, gay, straight, Christian, Jewish, Muslim, differently abled, plus-size, petite—everybody should be at your table. Everybody should be on your stage. Everybody should be on your staff. Everybody should be invited to your kid's birthday party. Everybody should be welcome in your church. Everybody should be invited over for dinner. Every single woman you know and every single one you don't could benefit from the truth that she is capable of something great. How is she ever going to believe that if nobody sets an example? How is she ever going to believe that if nobody cares enough to see it in her and speak the truth aloud?

The thing is, I believe there is magic in each and every one of you reading this. I know with every fiber of my being that if you all began to live more fully into that call on your heart—in spite of how scary and uncomfortable it feels at times—I know we would change the world. The incredible thing is, by embracing your calling and refusing to hide your glow, you wouldn't just make your world brighter. You'd light the way for the women who would come along behind you.

CONCLUSION

BELIEVE IN YOUR DANG SELF!

I'm pretty stinking fired up at this point. I almost went full-on bad language as I titled this last part, just so you'd know I was really and truly in beast mode on your behalf. But then I realized something: you have to already know that. If you don't realize that I am so on fire for you and your dreams and what you're going to accomplish in life, then we must just not know each other well enough yet.

I've devoted two books to the idea that you are in control of your life and capable of anything you set your heart and mind to. I've devoted my career and my company and therefore my life to creating content that reinforces that for you again and again. I believe in you. I believe in you so hard. I know that for many of you there aren't supportive family members or friends who will encourage you along this journey toward your goals, so please know, first and foremost, there's an enthusiastic mom of four living somewhere on a ranch in Texas that cannot wait to see what you do next!

Here's the second thing that you need to know—and why I stopped myself from adding cusswords to the title—it doesn't matter if I believe in you. It doesn't matter if I'm fired up on your behalf. I can write a thousand books and post a million inspiring Instagram stories, and none of it matters if you don't believe in yourself.

> I'm not going to be there tomorrow to tell you to get out of bed.
> I'm not going to be there next week when your shift gets cut at work and you don't know how you're going to make rent.
> I'm not going to be there when your family makes fun of you for trying to lose weight.
> I'm not going to be there when you fall off the wagon.
> I'm not going to be there when the shit hits the fan.
> I'm not going to be there when you quit on yourself.
> I'm not going to be there when you have to fight your way back.
> I'm not going to be there in your life dealing with your stuff.

You're going to be there every single day, so you better believe your life is worth fighting for!

It's as simple and as hard as that.

It means that you have to push through when you don't want to. It means that you have to find a way to not go binge eat. It means that you have to have a hard conversation with your sister about the way you're feeling. It means that you need to talk to your spouse about how you can have a stronger marriage. It means that you're going to have to do a lot of things that make you uncomfortable. It means that you're going to have to parent your kids instead of giving them what they want in order to keep the peace. It means that you're going to have to lead your team with the wisdom and determination of a great coach instead of the blind acceptance of a great cheerleader. It means that you're going to have to be your *own* coach as well as your own hype squad. It means that you're going to have to lead yourself well. It means that you're going to have to treat yourself with kindness but challenge yourself to become better!

There are a lot of things that you're going to have to do. None of them are easy, but all of them are simple. The easiest way, the fastest way, to get where you want to go is to not quit on yourself. When you're standing at the start of a long race, it feels very overwhelming. The idea of making it all the way to the finish line—without walking away this time—feels challenging. But it's possible, if you believe in yourself! You've heard that quote about doubt, right? Doubt will kill more dreams than failure ever will. But belief in yourself will give you the strength to get back up again and again.

You've got to take it one single day at a time. If an entire day feels too overwhelming, I'm going to ask you to take it an hour at a time and to keep reminding yourself: *This is who I am.*

Remember how we visualized the very best version of yourself, your dream version of who you are? This is who you are on the inside. Your soul has always known who you are. That's why it keeps tugging at your heart, begging you to listen. That's where your *what if* is coming from. That's what makes you wonder about what else is possible. That's what makes you sad when you don't get there, because you know, deep down in your belly, that a better version of you—a better version of this life—is waiting on the other side of that what if.

The real you is destined for something more . . . your version of more. This is who you were made to be, and the first step to making that vision a reality is to stop apologizing for having the dream in the first place. Like Lady Gaga says, baby, you were born this way. It's not your job to make yourself fit into anyone else's ideal. It's your job to start believing in who you are and what you're capable of. It's time to be yourself, unapologetically, and to show the world what happens when a woman challenges herself for greatness. It's time to stop apologizing for who you are. It's time to become who you were made to be.

ACKNOWLEDGMENTS

I always start my thank-yous at the beginning, and for my writing career that always resides with my agent Kevan Lyon. It's nearly unbelievable how far I've come as an author, and that is due in large part to your insight and wisdom—and the fact that you unabashedly dream-crush me every time I pitch you an idea involving world-building or magical realism. Someday, KL, someday.

Thank you to Brian Hampton and the team at Nelson Books and HarperCollins who took a chance on *Girl, Wash Your Face* and worked so hard alongside us to make it successful: Jenny Baumgartner, Jessica Wong, Brigitta Nortker, Stephanie Tresner, Sara Broun, and every single member of the sales team who championed my work to our retail partners and continues to answer my emails—even when they're annoying and likely overstepping.

Thank you to Jeff James and the team at HarperCollins Leadership for believing that a book that focuses on goal setting and achievement was the perfect sequel to a book that talked about hairy toes and incontinence.

As always, a big shout-out to the team at the Hollis Company, who remain the hardest working group in this industry or any other. We are small but mighty. We are the little engine that could. Don't let anyone tell you that a small group of determined people can't change the world—they already have.

Thank you, too, to my friend Annie Ludes, who illustrated the images in this book. A visual representation of my crazy ranting is no easy task, but Annie managed to knock it out of the park!

At the risk of sounding cheeseball, I want to take a moment to acknowledge my mentors. None of them have any idea who I am, but their work has given me the tools to change my life and my business and I am forever grateful for the guidance they have made available to dreamers like me. Dave Ramsey, Oprah Winfrey, John C. Maxwell, Keith J. Cunningham, Elizabeth Gilbert, Phil Knight, HRH Beyoncé Knowles Carter, Ed Mylett, Brendon Burchard, and, most especially, Tony Robbins have all been instrumental to me. If I have affected your life as an author, it is because these teachers have greatly affected my life as a student.

For my children, Jackson Cage, Sawyer Neeley, Ford Baker, and Noah Elizabeth. I hope the dreams you chase light your hearts on fire; I pray that I live my life in a way that makes you believe anything is possible.

And as always, I save the biggest and best thank-you for last. Dave Hollis is my touchstone, my cheerleader, and in many ways the caretaker I didn't have earlier in life. He's also now my business partner. In the midst of me writing this book we took a massive leap of faith—that didn't feel so massive to us. We moved our family and our company to Austin from Los Angeles. Dave quit a lucrative job at Disney after seventeen years and walked away from a title and a salary other people would kill to achieve. He did all this because he believes in this vision as much as I do. We want to build a company that gives people the tools and inspiration to change their lives. It's a grandiose ideal and one heck of a missional calling. I couldn't do this work without you, my love.

ABOUT THE AUTHOR

Rachel Hollis is a #1 *New York Times* and #1 *USA Today* bestselling author, a top business podcaster, and one of the most sought-after motivational speakers in the world. As a bestselling author and wildly successful lifestyle influencer, she has built a global social media fanbase in the millions. She's a proud working mama of four and a big fan of the small town in Texas hill country that the Hollis family calls home.

Hang out with her on Instagram (her favorite social!) @MsRachelHollis. To find out more about ALL the things, head to TheHollisCo.com.

NOTES

Part I: Excuses to Let Go Of

1. Google dictionary, s.v. "excuse," accessed September 15, 2018, https://www.google.com/search?active&q=Dictionary#dobs=excuse, taken from *Oxford Dictionaries*, s.v. "excuse," https://en.oxforddictionaries.com/definition/excuse.

Excuse 1: That's Not What Other Women Do

1. Brené Brown, "Listening to Shame," TED video, 20:32, talk presented at TED2012, March 2012, transcript, 13:20, https://www.ted.com/talks/brene_brown_listening_to_shame.

Excuse 9: Good Girls Don't Hustle

1. From the title of Laurel Thatcher Ulrich's book *Well-Behaved Women Seldom Make History* (New York: Knopf, 2007).

Part II: Behaviors to Adopt

1. Google dictionary, s.v. "behavior," accessed September 24, 2018, https://www.google.com/search?active&q=Dictionary#dobs=behavior, taken from *Oxford Dictionaries*, s.v. "behaviour," https://en.oxforddictionaries.com/definition/behaviour.

Behavior 1: Stop Asking Permission

1. *American Heritage Dictionary of the English Language*, 5th ed. (2016), s.v. "qualify," emphasis added.

Behavior 3: Embrace Your Ambition

1. *Oxford Dictionaries*, s.v. "ambition," accessed September 25, 2018, https://en.oxforddictionaries.com/definition/us/ambition.

Behavior 4: Ask for Help!

1. J. F. O. McAllister, "10 Questions for Madeleine Albright," *TIME*, January 10, 2008, http://content.time.com/time/magazine/article/0,9171,1702358,00.html.

Behavior 7: Learn to Say No

1. Original quote by Derek Sivers. Quoted at Jen Hatmaker (@jenhatmaker), "As you move into 2016 hoping for a saner schedule that prioritizes your actual life and keeps you focused on the things that matter the most," Facebook, January 4, 2016, https://www.facebook.com/jenhatmaker/posts/as-you-move-into-2016-hoping-for-a-saner-schedule-that-prioritizes-your-actual-l/881671191931877/.

Part III: Skills to Acquire

1. *Oxford Dictionaries*, s.v. "skill," accessed September 20, 2018, https://en.oxforddictionaries.com/definition/skill.

Skill 2: Confidence

1. Tara Sophia Mohr, "Why Women Don't Apply for Jobs Unless They're 100% Qualified," *Harvard Business Review*, August 25, 2014, https://hbr.org/2014/08/why-women-dont-apply-for-jobs-unless-theyre-100-qualified.

Skill 4: Effectiveness

1. Gary Keller and Jay Papasan, *The One Thing: The Surprisingly Simple Truth Behind Extraordinary Results* (Hudson Bend, TX: Bard Press, 2013).